NEW HALL
and Its Imitators

The Faber Monographs on Pottery and Porcelain

Former Editors: W. B. Honey *and* Arthur Lane
Present Editors: Sir Harry Garner *and* R. J. Charleston

∗

WORCESTER PORCELAIN AND LUND'S BRISTOL
by Franklin A. Barrett
DERBY PORCELAIN *by* Franklin A. Barrett *and* Arthur L. Thorpe
NINETEENTH-CENTURY ENGLISH POTTERY AND PORCELAIN
by Geoffrey Bemrose
ANCIENT AMERICAN POTTERY
by G. H. S. Bushnell and Adrian Digby
ROMAN POTTERY *by* R. J. Charleston
BLANC DE CHINE *by* P. J. Donnelly
ORIENTAL BLUE AND WHITE *by* Sir Harry Garner
CHINESE CELADON WARES *by* G. St. G. M. Gompertz
KOREAN CELADON AND OTHER WARES OF THE KORYO PERIOD
by G. St. G. M. Gompertz
KOREAN POTTERY AND PORCELAIN OF THE YI PERIOD
by G. St. G. M. Gompertz
NEW HALL AND ITS IMITATORS *by* David Holgate
GERMAN PORCELAIN *by* W. B. Honey
WEDGWOOD WARE *by* W. B. Honey
JAPANESE PORCELAIN *by* Soame Jenyns
JAPANESE POTTERY *by* Soame Jenyns
LATER CHINESE PORCELAIN *by* Soame Jenyns
ENGLISH PORCELAIN FIGURES OF THE EIGHTEENTH CENTURY
by Arthur Lane
FRENCH FAÏENCE *by* Arthur Lane
GREEK POTTERY *by* Arthur Lane
EARLY ISLAMIC POTTERY *by* Arthur Lane
LATER ISLAMIC POTTERY *by* Arthur Lane
ITALIAN PORCELAIN *by* Arthur Lane
MEDIEVAL ENGLISH POTTERY *by* Bernard Rackham
EARLY STAFFORDSHIRE POTTERY *by* Bernard Rackham
ITALIAN MAIOLICA *by* Bernard Rackham
ARTIST-POTTERS IN ENGLAND *by* Muriel Rose
ENGLISH CREAM-COLOURED EARTHENWARE
by Donald Towner
ENGLISH BLUE AND WHITE PORCELAIN
OF THE EIGHTEENTH CENTURY
by Bernard Watney
LONGTON HALL PORCELAIN *by* Bernard Watney

A. Jug decorated in enamels with monogram 'TC' in gold
New Hall, hard-paste, c. 1800; ht. 7¾ in. See pages 44 and 59

NEW HALL
and Its Imitators

by
DAVID HOLGATE

FABER AND FABER
3 Queen Square
London

First published in 1971
by Faber and Faber Limited
3 Queen Square London WC1
Printed in Great Britain by
Robert MacLehose and Company Limited
The University Press Glasgow

ISBN 0 571 08472 9

For
ROBIN

FOREWORD

Porcelain-manufacture in England has followed a different course from that in other countries. Whereas in Germany and Italy, and subsequently in France too, porcelain in the eighteenth century was made in a modified version of the 'true' or 'hard-paste' ware of the Orient, composed of china-clay and china-stone, in England various forms of 'soft-paste' porcelain were made. These in general gave way ultimately to a formula in which bone-ash played an important part as a constituent, this body finally evolving into the 'bone-china' which since the end of the eighteenth century has been, and still is, the distinctive English porcelain. The exception to this general development has been the isolated episode of the production of hard-paste porcelain, first at Plymouth, then at Bristol and finally at New Hall in Staffordshire. All these factories were related and succeeded one another. The New Hall concern itself was finally forced to give up hard-paste porcelain and to turn to the more economic bone-china body. Its recognition of commercial realities also affected form and decoration. Whereas the Bristol factory had aspired to styles as elaborate as those of any of its contemporaries, the New Hall factory, after an ambitious start, realised that its true market lay in the middle ranges of society. It therefore concentrated on simpler and cheaper styles of decoration for a wider clientele. In consequence, considerable quantities of New Hall porcelain have survived, and their relative simplicity has until fairly recently preserved them from the attentions of the collector and connoisseur. Now, when the search for early English porcelain of all sorts has become fiercely competitive, the balance has been redressed, and New Hall is eagerly collected. A comprehensive and discriminating book on the subject is therefore overdue.

Mr. Holgate has devoted many years of study and collecting activity to his chosen subject, but has not allowed his concentration to make him narrow-minded. A most useful feature of his book is that he does not exclude from his survey the wares of other factories often mistaken for those of New Hall. It should therefore prove particularly welcome to collectors who have turned to this field on account of the relative cheapness and availability of the porcelains of this type. He has rendered a great service in clarifying a hitherto confused chapter in the history of porcelain-making in England.

R.J.C.

CONTENTS

ILLUSTRATIONS

COLOUR PLATES
(*all New Hall*)

MONOCHROME PLATES
(*at the end of the book*)

Pieces with no acknowledgements are in the author's collection.
For the relevance of pattern numbers to the dating of pieces, see pages 63–64.

PREFACE

For many years New Hall has been the Cinderella of the early English porcelain factories. However, there are several reasons why it should be given a more important place in the history of English ceramics. It was the last of the few successful manufactories of porcelain to be established during the eighteenth century and it was the legal successor to the only English makers of hard-paste porcelain. Furthermore, although it was the second major Staffordshire firm to make porcelain (Longton Hall, 1749–60, being the first) it was without doubt responsible for the development of what is now one of the leading porcelain-manufacturing localities in the world.

The published literature does scant justice to New Hall's claim to fame. G. E. Stringer's book, *New Hall Porcelain* (1949), which attempted to give a descriptive picture of the contemporary scene as well as the china, is now out of date and G. E. A. Grey's chapter in *English Porcelain 1745–1850* (1965), which broke much new ground was, of necessity, a masterly compression of his wide knowledge. However, for the student and collector, Dr. T. A. Sprague's articles published in 1949 and 1950 in *Apollo* show the methodical approach of the scientist and give a sound background to the subject. Sprague was the first person to discuss the pitfalls and traps laid by the numerous factories which made and sold wares similar to those of New Hall. It has been my good fortune to be given free access to Dr. Sprague's papers and to be able to continue his work.

Excavation of the original Caughley site came at an opportune time and I have been able to confirm many of Sprague's predictions and show that a hard-paste body, similar to that pioneered by New Hall some fifteen years earlier, was made there. However, no evidence of a 'silver-shape' teapot came to hand and we must perforce look elsewhere for the makers of these.

In this book I have tried to give a comprehensive picture of the life of the New Hall China Manufactory and, by illustration, to show the full range of its wares. Study of the patterns and their numbers enables the reader to create a picture of the development of the potting shapes and styles of decoration during the period 1781 to 1835.

PREFACE

The section which deals with the 'imitators' is intended to show that many factories made tea-sets which can be mistaken for New Hall. I have not used the word to depreciate the products of these other factories nor do I wish to imply that Chamberlain and Minton only copied New Hall wares.

The book is intended for collectors of New Hall porcelain. It should help them to identify the wares and make them aware of the similar products made by other factories. I hope that some collectors may be stimulated to study the 'unknown' factories and to enlarge the present limited knowledge of them. I realise that in this field my work is far from complete but I firmly believe that publishing at this stage will do more good than remaining silent until everything is known. Research can never flourish in isolation.

Knowledge and understanding of a subject cannot be gained unaided. Throughout my work I have been fortunate to receive help, advice and co-operation from everyone I have met. In particular the friendship and help of Geoffrey Godden has been invaluable. Some of my debts can never be repaid adequately. Private collectors will find my acknowledgements with the illustrations of their pieces and I hope that many dealers will be pleased when they recognize the treasures which they put on one side for me. I am particularly grateful for the many conversations I have had with Geoffrey Grey. Museum staff have always been helpful and I hope that they will accept the acknowledgements which accompany the illustrations as an expression of my thanks. The high proportion of illustrations from the collection in the City Museum and Art Gallery at Stoke-on-Trent is an indication of my debt to Arnold Mountford and his staff, who have devoted much of their time and energy to helping me. Pieces without acknowledgements are in my own collection.

I owe a large debt to Dr. E. J. W. Whittaker who gave me access to the laboratory facilities of the Oxford University Department of Geology. Through his generosity and help I was able to carry out the analyses using electron diffraction techniques. The useful application of these techniques to the analysis of ceramic bodies was originally explained to me by Mavis Bimson.

It has been a pleasure to have this book published by Faber and Faber for whom Giles de la Mare has always been a patient help. Kate Foster gave much assistance and help before the manuscript was destined to become a monograph. This final form could not have been achieved without the careful assistance of Robert Charleston. I am grateful to the whole team.

Finally, I must thank Manna Sprague, whose enthusiasm and help have been a constant source of encouragement.

Part I

NEW HALL

1

THE PATENT COMES TO
STAFFORDSHIRE

The history of the New Hall China Manufactory forms a large part of the history of the manufacture of so-called hard-paste porcelain in England and a small part of that of the manufacture of bone-china. It is curious that England has been the 'odd man out' as far as porcelain making is concerned. It is one of the few countries in which the production of hard-paste porcelain has not become established, so that nowadays whilst almost everyone else makes a hard-paste body England makes bone-china. This is a porcelain whose body contains bone ash—a material first used by Bow.

Study of comprehensive collections of eighteenth-century English porcelain gives the justified impression that the majority of wares were made in soft-paste. But it would be wrong to draw the conclusion that the early English manufacturers were only interested in soft-paste porcelain and that their interest in hard-paste was aroused towards the end of the century. It is generally accepted that the first English porcelain was made about 1745 (a piece of Chelsea porcelain dated 1745 is known, and the Frye patent taken out for the Bow factory was enrolled in 1744) and was soft-paste. To balance this it is certain that William Cookworthy, the Plymouth chemist, began to take an interest in hard-paste porcelain about this time also and commenced his research into its manufacture.

Cookworthy wrote to a surgeon friend in Cornwall on 30th May 1745:[1]

> 'I had lately with me, the person who discovered the china earth. He had with him several samples of the china ware, which I think were equal to the Asiatic. It was found on the back of Virginia, where he has been in quest of mines; and having read Du Halde, he discovered both the petuntze and kaolin. . . .'

His research took a long time to bear fruit, however, and it was not

[1] John Prideaux, *Relics of William Cookworthy*, London, 1853.

3

until 17th March 1768 that he took out and was granted a patent for the manufacture of hard-paste porcelain. This then is really the beginning of our story because it is this patent which was transferred to Richard Champion at Bristol in 1774. After a bitter struggle in Parliament, Champion had the life of the patent extended until 1796 and it was the extended patent which was sold to the group of Staffordshire potters who founded the New Hall China Manufactory.

William Cookworthy was the first person in England to discover where to obtain the two basic raw materials (china-clay and china-stone) that the Chinese used for making porcelain. He found them in Cornwall on Carloggas moor, which was the property of Mr. Thomas Pitt (later to become Lord Camelford), and when he had discovered how to convert them into porcelain he took out the patent which reserved to him the sole right of manufacture. Soon after (in 1770), he was granted a ninety-nine years' lease on Pitt's land which would supply the raw materials—in fact this was probably an extension of an earlier agreement. There was a covenant '. . . that he, the said Thomas Pitt and his heirs should not during the term permit any Moor Stone or Gravel, being on any estate or land belonging to him to be raised and used for the making of porcelain and china other than by virtue of this lease upon penalty of £20 for every ton.' The covenant and the lease were to cause Richard Champion, the Bristol merchant, considerable trouble in later years.

Richard Champion, a Quaker like Cookworthy, was a successful businessman but, unlike Cookworthy, he had no scientific background or experience in porcelain making. Josiah Wedgwood in a much-quoted letter to his partner Bentley laid great emphasis on this last point. Champion, when he bought Cookworthy's patent, worked hard in his efforts to make fine, hard-paste porcelain a commercial success and, as we have seen, in 1775 even had the patent protection extended until 1796.

The extension was bitterly opposed by Wedgwood on behalf of the Staffordshire potters, not just because it prevented other potters from making hard-paste porcelain but because it restricted the use of the raw materials in any ceramic product. The details of the battle are told in other books and need not be repeated here;[1] the outcome was protection for Champion's porcelain manufacture coupled with freedom for any potter to use the raw materials in a non-translucent product. It was an important concession because it allowed the Staffordshire potters to import the materials and acquire skill and practice in handling them. It also led to the discovery of alternative sources of supply which resulted, as always, in price competition.

[1] Ll. Jewitt, *The Ceramic Art of Great Britain*, 1878, and G. E. Stringer, *New Hall Porcelain*, 1949.

The cost of extending the patent was high and probably dashed any hopes which Champion had of making his manufacture of porcelain profitable. Production was at a low ebb in 1778 and Champion began to seek a way out. Wedgwood contemptuously talked about buying raw materials from him at low prices but Champion never suffered this humiliation. Wedgwood must have been greatly surprised when in 1780 Champion approached him with a proposition for making china in Staffordshire. On 12th November 1780 Wedgwood wrote to his partner Bentley:[1]

'Amongst other things Mr. Champion of Bristol has taken me up near two days. He is come amongst us to dispose of his secret—His patent etc. and, who could have believed it? has chosen me for his friend and confidante. I shall not deceive him for I really feel much for his situation. A wife and eight children (to say nothing of himself) to provide for, and out of what I fear will not be thought of much value here—The secret of China making. He tells me he has sunk fifteen thousand pounds in this gulf, and his idea is now to sell the whole art, mystery, and patent for six, and he is now trying a list of names I have given him of the most substantial and enterprising potters amongst us, and will acquaint me with the event.

I gave him reasons why I could not be concerned in such a partnership which I believe were satisfactory even to himself.'

Whenever a student of New Hall reads this letter for the first time, his heart rises. The whole story of the beginning of New Hall is going to be told by a contemporary writer. Such hopes are dashed because the letter was the last one to be written to Bentley: he died some two weeks later.

Connected facts about the Bristol–New Hall changeover are at a premium. Like the Wedgwood letter already quoted many promising leads never reach fulfilment. Nevertheless, the problems which faced Champion can be outlined, and their solution conjectured.

Champion had obviously decided that his Bristol works should close and that he should make the best provision for himself and his family. He was originally a merchant and more recently a potter, so that probably he thought of going to Staffordshire to make a living from one or both of these activities. On the other hand, he had always moved in good company and often among politicians, and so something similar to his final career as Paymaster to the Forces, which later took him to London and America, may have been in his mind.

[1] This letter is reproduced by kind permission of the museum at Josiah Wedgwood and Sons, Ltd.

The process for making hard-paste porcelain and the patent protection until 1796 was obviously something which could be sold, but the simple offer could only be made if Champion completely severed any direct connections with the patent. His agreements with Pitt and Cookworthy tied him to buy raw materials from Pitt only, whose price was higher than some of the alternative sources, and to pay Cookworthy or his heirs a levy on the materials used. What a problem for Champion and any prospective buyers! In an attempt to modify some part of these agreements Champion approached the executors of Cookworthy. He wrote first to Mr. Fox, who knew their cousin Mr. Harrison.[1]

After a brief correspondence Champion wrote to Mr. George Harrison, at No. 5 Fish Street Hill, Henbury, Bristol, explaining very clearly the position in which he found himself. This letter is actually dated 3rd September 1780 but presumably it should be 1781 since it follows other letters dated 1781.

'Sir,

Our mutual friend Mr. Fox has given me your letter to him of the 22nd August: in consequence of which I shall give you my Sentiments upon the Occasion, principally in the manner I did to him. When I first went into Staffordshire in the Spring my views were considerably more enlarged than they are at present. I intended to have established a large work, and if Mr. Wedgwood would have supported it, I might have done it. But this opposition prevented me and I have now entered into an agreement with ten Potters only, who if they like the Manufactory on its Establishment in the County are to give me a certain sum for liberty to use it in their own works, but I have also liberty to sell to any other I please on the original Plan for a Company, there was a clause designed to be inserted, that every Potter who belonged to it, should have on payment of a certain fine, liberty to make China in his Works.

In this situation I naturally looked to some Advantages from the sale of Materials but the high price of them, compared with those of Trethewys (Twelve guineas a year) and Carthews equally cheap, made me have very little hopes of advantage.

The Potters who knew the prices and your claim made this a capital objection to a Company, I therefore laid the case fairly before Mr. Pitt, who was equally concerned with me, with respect to the use of his Materials. He wrote me that he would make any reasonable Abatement.

[1] A transcription of this letter was made by W. J. Pountney and is preserved by the Bristol Archives Office (accession number 14790). It was published first by R. J. Charleston in the *Connoisseur*, April 1956, p. 186.

The case stands thus with all of us, I have a lease from Mr. Pitt for 99 years, you have the same Claim from me as he receives for the Materials, but I carry on the smallest work, the advantages you will either receive will be trifling. Again, if I carry on no work, the Lease falls into Mr. Pitt's hands, he may make what Bargain he pleases with fresh Leasees, or sell his Materials, and your Claim sinks in course, as it only exists with my Lease, which is Determinable on my carrying on the work or not.

Mr. Pitt is certainly in the worst Situation if I do, because the tax which I consented to lay on his Materials by my Agreement with Mr. Cookworthy, makes the Materials cost so much (and being a perpetuity without a possibility of it ceasing) that in its present state it must naturally throw the sale of Materials into other hands to his great Injury.

The Remidy comes next. I wish to reap Advantage naturally from the sale of Materials. I wish equally for you. Mr. Pitt must do the same. But strong as all our Wishes are, I see no Method than your consenting to restrain your claim to a certain period or such a certain price per annum as we can agree on. But to settle this arises fresh Difficulties. Hitherto what has arisen to you has been very trifling. In future if I could render the Materials tolerably cheap, it may increase. But if this is not to be done, it must be a total loss to all you and me, as Mr. Pitt may by my not being (able) to carry on the Work, enter into fresh Agreements.

At present he seems willing to agree to reasonable Terms. You will please always to carry this in your View, that the Potters will buy when[1] they please, and that there is no other way of engaging them than by selling cheap.

I have said sufficient on this occasion to make you Master of the subject, when you have considered it, you will be so good as to write me your Sentiments.

I beg to be remembered particularly to Mrs. Harrison and your sister Lydia who is with you and that you will believe me to be your sincere friend and servant

Richard Champion.'

We have to draw our own conclusions from the letter and later events, for no more facts emerge. Doubtless Wedgwood's lack of interest curtailed Champion's ambitions, as also did the restrictions on the source of materials and the Cookworthy surcharge.

It is possible that Cookworthy's heirs reduced or renounced their due but Pitt had little to lose by holding out. An objective assessment,

---

[1] Presumably this should be 'where'.

however, suggests that the most likely course would be for Champion to sell the patent outright and possibly act as the manager. In this way the new Company would be freed from any restrictions on the source of the raw materials. Champion's stay in Staffordshire was only from 5th November 1781 to 8th April 1782, when he suddenly left for London to take up a political post. His stay would have been long enough only to supervise a few successful firings of ware (a likely stipulation to any deal) and hardly long enough to establish manufacture. But would he have taken his family with him to Staffordshire if he had intended to stay only a few months before seeking another way of life? I think it likely that he began as the manager of the concern, since the Company appointed John Daniel in this capacity when he left, and that the political post came unexpectedly.

2

THE PARTNERS

When agreement was finally reached the number of substantial and enterprising potters appears to have dwindled from ten to six—or seven if Joshua Heath, Charles Bagnall's partner, was actually involved. None of the original New Hall documents has come to light so that the names of the partners have had to be culled from references in advertisements and the records of other factories. So far, no direct reference has been found to Joshua Heath's being a partner.

In later chapters I shall write about the life of the factory and its wares but it seems timely now to look at the men who started the enterprise and nurtured it until it became an established success.

JOHN TURNER (born 1738, died 1787)

The son of a lawyer, John Turner was a first-generation potter. Even so he was one of the most skilful and enterprising potters in Staffordshire. His stoneware, caneware, basaltes and jasperware products stand alongside those of Wedgwood with pride. He was successful. Why did he help to found New Hall and yet retire before the venture had really begun? Some of his activities and achievements in this connection are enigmas.

In 1775, with Josiah Wedgwood, he represented the Staffordshire potters in opposing the extension of Champion's hard-paste patent. Then in 1781 he was a member of the consortium of potters who negotiated with Champion and bought this same hard-paste patent—an apparent *volte face*. However, it has been suggested that Turner was sent by the Staffordshire potters to keep an eye on Wedgwood's activities rather than to fight for their belief in their freedom to use the raw materials.[1]

No doubt Turner, like many potters, yearned to make porcelain, and, being adventurous and capable, he took the opportunity when it arose.

A document which was amongst the New Hall property deeds when

[1] B. Hillier, *The Turners of Lane End*, 1965, p. 34.

G. E. Stringer wrote his book in 1949 gives the following information (page 11):

'Manor of Newcastle-under-Lyme
Surrender of 7th July, 1779

"To this Court comes John Hollins of Newcastle aforesaid, mercer, Ralph Baddely of Shelton, potter, and Thomas Smith of Penkhull, gent., all of the County of Stafford, and surrender into the hands of the Lord of the said Manor all that messuage called Shelton Hall with the little croft thereto adjoining and all potworks, barns, stables, gardens, hereditaments and appurtenances to the same belonging, and also all those closes and pieces of land to the same adjoining, late the estate of Alice Dalton, and called The Hall Meadows, the Middle Field, the Aslams Patch, the Clover Field, Miles' Meadow, the Near Bryans Wood, the Middle Bryans Wood and the Further Bryans Wood, including the oatfield and all ways, watercourses and appurtenances to the same belonging, To the use and behoof of John Turner of Lane End in the County of Stafford, Potter, for the term of 99 years if Humphrey Palmer late of Hanley, potter, shall so long live".'

We do not know what was in Turner's mind when he leased this property but Mr. Stringer suggests that it was done in preparation for making porcelain in partnership with Champion: for we do know that Turner was one of the group of potters who combined to buy the Champion hard-paste patent and that both he and Keeling withdrew when Champion left to further his political career. We do not know why Turner and Keeling left but it is curious to find that when Turner left he allowed the remaining potters to use Shelton Hall for the manufacture of their hard-paste porcelain.

Turner's career after this episode does not come into the story of New Hall but he still had ambitions to make porcelain and, since there are marked examples, we know that these ambitions were fulfilled. The full range of his porcelain has not yet been discovered and there is a possibility that he was responsible for the products made by the unknown Factory X; this will be discussed in more detail on page 100.

ANTHONY KEELING (born 1738, died 1815)

Anthony Keeling was the other partner to leave the Company in 1782. He had married into the potting world in 1760, when he married Ann Booth, the daughter of the famous potter Enoch Booth. Keeling obviously partnered Booth before his marriage, since on 6th December 1759 there is mention in the *Edinburgh Evening*

Courant of a saleroom/warehouse business in their joint names. After Booth's death Keeling took over the Cliff Bank Works at Tunstall and later built the Phoenix Works, where in 1781 the first New Hall porcelain was made. He was clearly a capable and experienced potter.

It is not known how New Hall retailed their porcelain but I am inclined to believe that they had warehouses in some provincial cities. In fact I once thought it possible that one of the reasons for Keeling's presence on the board was his warehouse in Edinburgh. However, this was not the case, because in 1775 (1st April and 18th November) newspaper notices appeared saying that he had decided to give up his business in Edinburgh, and the stock was sold. There were no further notices of a warehouse or saleroom in his name after that date although his name did appear in the street directories until 1782–83.

The date 1775–76 for the closure of the Edinburgh warehouse assumes more significance if coupled with the fact that Keeling owed money (£6 3s. 3d.) to John Wedgwood, 'earth potter' of the Big House, Burslem, for wares supplied. Wedgwood's account book shows that during the period 1761 to 1775 Anthony Keeling bought spoons, melons and 'unfired wares' from him. It seems likely that Keeling was in some financial difficulty in 1775, hence the Edinburgh sale. Perhaps in 1782 his finances were not stable enough to allow him to continue with the New Hall Company.

After leaving the New Hall Company Keeling continued to make Queen's ware and Egyptian black until he retired to Liverpool in 1810 and died there in 1815.

The New Hall partnership embraced many religions. Samuel Hollins was a pillar of the Anglican Church, Jacob Warburton was a Roman Catholic, John Daniel was a Free Thinker and Anthony Keeling was for many years the principal supporter of a place of worship on his premises, for a society of the sect of Christians called Sandemanians.[1]

SAMUEL HOLLINS (born 1748, died 1820)

Samuel Hollins was a respected and respectable member of the community. He was the sixth son in a family of nine children and was the father of six children by his first marriage.

His father's (Richard Hollins) generous help towards the building of the first St. John's Church in Hanley was continued by his own philanthropy in the building of another Hanley Church in 1787 and the Parsonage House in 1813. Samuel Hollins' stock stood so high that in 1796 he became the Mayor of Hanley and Shelton. Such

[1] Ll. Jewitt, *op. cit.*, vol. 2, p. 303.

integrity at the head of the New Hall Company must have been of inestimable value.

Although he inherited a share in two coal mines (Birches Head Mine and Roe Hurst Mine) from his father, Samuel Hollins was a potter. His factory at Cauldon Canal, Vale Pleasant, Shelton, made cream-coloured earthenware and 'red china'; the most frequently found products are dark-red stonewares, some of which bear the impressed mark 'S. HOLLINS'. There is no connection between these pieces and those marked 'T & J HOLLINS' which were made independently by his two nephews.

The production of pottery at Vale Pleasant was carried on whilst he was a member of the New Hall Company so that when he bought a 'messuage, mill and other freehold lands and hereditaments, lying within the Manor or Lordship of Bucknall', from a William Adams for £1000, the mill was probably used in the preparation of materials for both factories.

It is one of the tragedies of New Hall that there was no family continuity within the company. There was only one son amongst Samuel Hollins' six children and he, Thomas, went to Manchester, where he was styled as a 'merchant'. It was to this son that the Hollins share in the New Hall Company (valued at £5,975) was bequeathed in 1820. On the other hand, one of his daughters, Ann, married Herbert Minton, but they had the Minton firm to work for and maintain.

The final irony, so far as New Hall is concerned, is that Samuel Hollins' grandson, Michael Daintry Hollins (born 1815), although qualifying in Manchester as a surgeon, gave up his career to become a partner in the Minton firm with his uncle Herbert.

JACOB WARBURTON (born 1741, died 1826)

PETER WARBURTON (born 1773, died 1813)

JOHN DANIEL (born 1756, died 1821)

Jacob Warburton was the second son of John Warburton and Ann Daniel. John Daniel was the nephew of Ann Daniel. The two families can be considered together when studying their part in the history of New Hall.

The potting traditions of the Warburton and Daniel families were long, both names being known in potting circles in the seventeenth century. At the beginning of the eighteenth century Joseph Warburton (1694–1752) was potting in Hot Lane and was considered to be one of the most important manufacturers. His son John (1720–61) married Ann Daniel, herself a master potter, who survived him by thirty-seven years. After her husband's death Ann carried on a very successful and important enamelling business with her son Thomas under the title 'Ann Warburton and Son'.

Jacob Warburton, Ann's second son, had his own pottery at Cobridge when he became one of the proprietors of the New Hall China Manufactory. Although he probably continued to run his own pottery, and Jewitt says that he also succeeded his mother in the family potworks, his main energies were obviously spent on New Hall.

Simeon Shaw, the ceramic historian and chemist, knew Jacob Warburton well and wrote of him in glowing terms mentioning also his literary and linguistic talent. Even allowing for exaggeration by Shaw we can see that the Warburton name was respected. Josiah Wedgwood would not have invited him to act as an arbitrator against Humphrey Palmer if it had been otherwise. Not long before 1810 Jacob Warburton retired from New Hall in favour of his son Peter, and although he may have kept a fatherly eye on the works for a short time, in 1814 he married for the second time (*Staffordshire Advertiser*, 28th May 1814) and retired to Ford Green House.

Peter and Francis Warburton were Jacob's sons and they potted together at Bleak Hill, Cobridge—perhaps the family works—producing a good quality creamware. Francis did not stay in the business and the partnership was dissolved in 1802 (*Staffordshire Advertiser*, 3rd April 1802), leaving Peter to carry on. Peter replaced his father as a New Hall partner and in 1810 was involved in the buying of the estate. However, his most important achievement was the discovery of the method of transfer-printing in gold for which he took out a patent in 1810. His death in 1813 at the age of forty was a severe blow to New Hall. Peter Warburton married Mary Emery, whose father Francis is said to have been the decorating manager at New Hall. This may be true but there is no further evidence. Jewitt refers to a Mr. F. J. Emery as working for T. Furnival and Son before becoming the proprietor of the Bleak Hill works.[1] If Mr. F. J. Emery was Peter Warburton's father-in-law it is possible that he became the proprietor of Bleak Hill works in 1813 on Peter's death.

Turning to John Daniel, who was employed as the manager of the New Hall Company when Champion left, we find that his forbears played a large part in the introduction of plaster of paris moulds and in the development of on-glaze enamelling. His ability, loyalty and competence can be assessed by the fact that he was the New Hall manager for about forty years, until in 1821 he was succeeded by

[1] Ll. Jewitt, *op. cit.*, vol. 2, p. 295.

John Tittensor. In the last decade of the eighteenth century his name appeared in announcements alongside the names of the original partners so it seems that during this period he became a partner as well as the manager—unless this latter post gave him an *ex officio* seat on the board.

The announcement of his death in the *Staffordshire Advertiser* (27th June 1821) refers to him as a 'proprietor of the long established concern the New Hall China Works'. He is also referred to as a Free Thinker, and as such was buried in unconsecrated ground.

CHARLES BAGNALL (born 1747, died 1814)

Although Charles Bagnall is recorded as being a potter, and partner to Joshua Heath, it seems likely that he acted more as a business man on the New Hall board. Like Samuel Hollins he was a respected member of the community and subscribed to the rebuilding of St. John's Church. In 1784, together with other partners, he attended the first Mayor's Feast at Hanley.

On the business side, a lease of the Carloggas Pit (on Lord Camelford's land) was taken out in 1795 in the name of Bagnall and Co. This has been thought to be a pseudonym for the New Hall Company since the mine was previously leased to them when Champion's patent was procured. Then, when these agreements were reviewed, Bagnall took part in the negotiations. In 1799 he signed as a partner in the Hendra Company.[1] He was also a coalmaster, being one of the many partners in Samuel Perry and Co., who owned the New Hays and Sneyd Green Collieries. In 1797 this partnership was dissolved. Adding to the diversity of his business activities, Bagnall is listed as a lead merchant in 1800.

Searches in advertisements and records of the New Hall Company show that some time between 1804 and 1810 he retired,[2] perhaps in 1807, when he was sixty years old.

WILLIAM CLOWES

Comparatively little is known about William Clowes although his name appears on New Hall documents until about 1813. Apart from signing the Hendra Company agreement in 1799 the most important documents which he signed were the New Hall deeds when its buildings and estate were bought in 1810.

Clowes lived and worked in Longport making earthenware and

---

[1] The Hendra Company was formed by a group of Staffordshire potters to work a clay mine at Hendra Common in Cornwall, and thus obtain china-clay and -stone for their own use, and for sale to other manufacturers.

[2] See page 22.

basaltes. Later, during the last decade of the eighteenth century, he had two partners, Henshall and Williamson. It is perhaps worth noting that Robert Williamson married the widow of James Brindley the engineer, and one of their sons married William Clowes' daughter Anne. Mrs. Williamson's maiden name was Henshall, so that it was probably her brother who was the third partner in the firm of Clowes, Henshall and Williamson.

NOTE ON SOURCES USED IN CHAPTER 2

The sources for the information given in this chapter are the books by W. A. Pitt, Simeon Shaw, J. Ward, Llewellyn Jewitt, J. C. Wedgwood, G. E. Stringer, B. Hillier and R. M. Barton and the *Apollo* article by R. G. Haggar listed in the Bibliography, and advertisements in the *Staffordshire Advertiser* and the *Edinburgh Evening Courant*.

3

THE NEW HALL CHINA
MANUFACTORY 1781-1835

I often wonder why these potters ventured into the world of porcelain. What was their vision? Answers to these questions are pure speculation but they can be based upon the foundation of fact presented by the porcelain itself and the contemporary scene.

The Industrial Revolution, which was to change irrevocably the entire structure of the working world and the lives of the middle class, began about twenty years before the New Hall partners bought Richard Champion's patent. I think these potters saw the opening of a new and growing market for porcelain tea-wares. An increase in wealth and a rising standard of living took place in many families and, although they may not have been able to afford silver or the most expensive porcelain tea-services, nevertheless they may no longer have been satisfied with the common creamware. Was it this, then? I believe that the New Hall partners foresaw a market for simple and comparatively cheap gilded and coloured tea-sets; nothing so expensive as the finest Worcester porcelain and yet more colourful than blue-and-white, more refined than earthenware.

These potters must also have been aware of the increase in the habit and custom of tea drinking. During the eighteenth century the price of tea was gradually reduced and finally, in 1784, the tax on it was removed. Although this latter point may seem to us in this tax-ridden age to be the ultimate blessing, it has been suggested that in fact it made little difference to the quantity of tea which was consumed. So much was smuggled into the country that only the legality of its use was affected!

Since this new market was growing in the heart of England, that is the midlands and the industrial north, a convenient site for the works was obviously Staffordshire. From there trade routes would be short and the wares could be sold easily by travellers. Perhaps they felt no need to make a special effort to win London trade. So far no evidence has been found of a London showroom selling New Hall china although Abbott and Mist had a warehouse in Fleet Street,

B. Tea-caddy and plate painted in enamels by Fidelle Duvivier. New Hall, hard-paste, c. 1782–7; ht. of caddy 4 in. See page 59

where John Turner's Staffordshire wares were sold. It is mentioned
elsewhere (page 11) that Anthony Keeling had a warehouse in Edinburgh but it was closed before New Hall began. On the other hand,
some tea-sets have been noted which bore the marks 'Cotton, High
Street, Edinburgh' and 'E. Cotton, Edinburgh'. It would appear that
these sets were sold by Elijah Cotton, who had a 'stone, glass and
china warehouse' in High Street, Edinburgh about 1806–10. In the
1820's the Herculaneum Warehouse in Duke Street, Liverpool, purchased large quantities of New Hall; obviously this was for retail or
export.

The exact location of a factory was very important for commercial
success. Primarily it needed to have both raw materials at hand and
good transport facilities. All the existing porcelain makers like Bristol,
Caughley, Lowestoft and Worcester were well served by water-borne
transport which enabled them safely to import their materials and
export their wares. Clay and coal occur abundantly in Staffordshire
and to the potter coal is the more useful. At first sight this may
seem unlikely but it is true. Although a simple piece of underglaze
blue-and-white porcelain may receive only two firings (about forty-
eight hours for the biscuit and fourteen hours for the glaze) it is
possible for a finely decorated piece of porcelain to be fired six times.
In making one ton of finished ware a potter might use ten to twelve
tons of coal. Thus many of the Staffordshire potbanks were built
beside a coal mine rather than a clay pit. In any case Staffordshire
clay was not used for making porcelain.

In the second half of the eighteenth century transport throughout
the country improved. In 1762, when a petition was presented to
Parliament, the conditions described were appalling. Clay and stone
could be carried by barge either on the Rivers Mersey and Weaver
to Winsford in Cheshire or up the River Trent from Hull to Willington in Derbyshire. A pack horse or carriage had to be used for the
remainder of the journey (about sixteen miles from Winsford and
about thirty miles from Willington). No wonder there was agitation
for turnpike roads. Yet when these were made they were not sufficient
to cope with the developing industry. In 1777, the water link between
the Trent and Mersey (named originally the Grand Trunk Canal) was
opened and from that year the real industrial importance and
prosperity of Staffordshire grew. At last supplies of raw materials
could be easily and cheaply transported;[1] the fragile final product
could be carried gently and safely.

[1] J. C. Wedgwood, in *Staffordshire Pottery and its History*, 1913, writes that
only nine years after the canal was opened, the freight for general goods was
1¼d. per ton per mile, or less than one-seventh of the cost before the canal was cut.

No doubt the triumphant success of the Grand Trunk Canal was a major factor both in Champion's decision to turn to the Potteries for help, and in the acceptance by our group of potters of the challenge which their vision presented.

This Canal enabled Staffordshire potters to increase their exports, which even in 1765, before its construction, exceeded the home consumption. North America, France, Holland, Sweden and Germany were all good markets. Unfortunately, as the proportion of exports rose the ceramic industry began to suffer from the effects of international squabbles, with their spiteful blockades and retaliatory import duties. Balance of payments problems and protection were as real in the eighteenth century as they are today.

It is not known whether the New Hall partners considered building up an export trade. Whether they did or not, their early years must have been affected by the American War which caused much distress in Staffordshire. In fact the hard times and recessions in trade caused by this war must have increased the problems of the new-born Company. In 1783 rioting occurred and troops had to be called out to restore order.

America was not the only export market. Europe was a closer neighbour and the earthenware manufacturers strove to sell their products across the Channel. There were high tariffs to contend with, barriers which the superior quality of the Staffordshire cream-ware were able to surmount. Some of these barriers, especially those in France and Germany, had been raised because England had raised similar ones against the importation of European porcelain.

A Commercial Treaty with France was signed in 1786 which once more opened the doors for trade. Staffordshire seems to have benefited very much from this Treaty and we must remember that Josiah Wedgwood played a part in putting forward the potters' views to the authorities. Trade boomed and the value of exports rose.

The French wars, which lasted on and off until 1815, had comparatively little effect upon the Staffordshire potters until 1806, when Napoleon issued from Berlin his famous decrees declaring the British Isles to be in a state of blockade. Unfortunately American ships became involved in the retaliatory English blockade and they too closed their ports to English goods.

Between 1806 and 1812 the export trade declined seriously and many potters became bankrupt. The New Hall partners must have had great courage to buy their lease in 1810 and then, between 1812 and 1814, change over from their proven hard-paste to the new bone-china body.

Probably the nadir was in 1812. A slight improvement in trade followed until peace came with France and Napoleon was finally routed. Peace, and the cumulative effects of the Industrial Revolution, hoisted Great Britain in 1815 to the brink of an unprecedented period of greatness and prosperity. Alas, this greatness did not mean eternal industrial prosperity. The immediate boom was short-lived and followed by economic crisis. Thereafter it was a case of fluctuating recovery.

The problems of transport and supply of raw materials had been largely solved by the turn of the century, but labour difficulties and low wages caused increasing unrest; the cost of living had risen but the level of wages had not. As articulate leaders arose workers became united and although they were beaten in their first efforts to strike in 1825, the time was soon to come when they were not to be quelled. The ten years from 1830 was a period of great unrest and strife in Staffordshire.

The life of New Hall must be seen within this economic picture, largely determined by international politics. Its porcelain was probably made for the home market, though since it was part of a close-knit community whose products were exported widely, complete independence was impossible. To a certain extent both good times and bad must have diffused from one factory to another.

The Potteries were not enjoying prosperity when the group of Staffordshire potters bought Champion's patent in 1781, and the situation deteriorated, if anything, when they left Keeling's factory and acquired the lease of Shelton Hall. The name Shelton Hall was not unique, because when Mr. Whitehead built it there were already two other mansions with this title. The partners probably called it New Hall because it was the most modern of the three halls, but it must be realised that the firm's business title was 'Hollins, Warburton and Company'. In 1812, by Act of Parliament, Shelton was absorbed by Hanley so that the Company's address became New Hall, Hanley, Staffordshire.

Although the short time at Keeling's factory in Tunstall, before the move to Shelton Hall, served as a preliminary limbering-up period, the withdrawal of the original patent owner, Richard Champion, and the two experienced potters, John Turner and Anthony Keeling, must have retarded the real start. To replace these men Jacob Warburton's cousin John Daniel was employed as the manager.

Shelton Hall was well situated for materials and transport. There were several wharves and warehouses on the Grand Trunk Canal and from one of these, Etruria wharf, a horse railway ran up to the centre of Hanley. Although this did not run directly to the Hall any journey from it would probably be on the level or even slightly downhill. By this means clay and stone could be carried.

The canal would not be needed for carrying coal. Apparently some was mined on the New Hall site, for Mr. Stringer records finding in 1912 a pit shaft beneath the floor of one of the buildings.[1] The coal mine interests held by both Samuel Hollins and Charles Bagnall which were not far away must also have served the factory.

The cost of china-clay and china-stone had always been a thorn in Champion's side, especially when he tried to sell the patent. Despite the facility with which other potters seemed able to buy these raw materials more cheaply, New Hall were probably forced to take over Champion's lease from Lord Camelford. There were conditions attached to this lease for both sides. Lord Camelford was not to sell the materials to any other potters, whilst the lessees would be considered to default if they left the rent unpaid for 60 days or failed to work the pit for two years. It is clear that New Hall did not comply fully, since in 1789 Lord Camelford sought legal advice on unpaid rent and apparent neglect of the mines. Although Camelford was unable to foreclose, the legal enquiries stirred the lessees, who restarted mining operations—perhaps under a revised agreement. In 1795 after further investigations the lease was granted to Bagnall and Co. (i.e. New Hall) until 1796, when the patent expired and a junior Lord Camelford, who succeeded to the title in 1793, came of age.

Once the patent had expired, competition in buying china-clay and -stone must have increased, and New Hall probably felt that they had greater freedom in choosing their source of materials. In 1799 they took out a lease on Hendra Common and almost immediately, with Thomas Minton, took a leading part in the formation of the Hendra Company. This company, which also included Wedgwood and Adams, continued as an effective supplier of materials until well into the nineteenth century. It did not fail until about 1839.

Ball-clay, so named because it was sold in large balls, was used by the potters as well as china-clay. Although less pure than the china-clay it restores to a mixture some of the strength and plasticity which has been refined out of the kaolin. The principal source of ball-clay was the Isle of Purbeck in Dorset, and New Hall joined with many other Staffordshire potters after 1791 in buying it from William Pike of Chuddleigh. It is interesting to speculate whether this contract led to Ann Warburton (daughter of Jacob Warburton) being introduced to her husband. She married William Pike in 1803.

Once the clays and stone arrived in Shelton they had to be prepared for use. The traditional powers, wind and water, were used for mills

[1] G. E. Stringer, *op. cit.*, p. 57.

when the factory started but steam power was soon to be introduced to the Potteries. Boulton's Sun and Planet engines were installed by Josiah Wedgwood at Etruria in 1784 and 1793 and later by other manufacturers. In New Hall's early days grinding was probably done in the Bucknall mills which Samuel Hollins bought in 1788. Bagnall's lease on the Sneyd Mills in 1792 would help to increase the output of prepared materials, some of which New Hall sold to other potters. There is no evidence that they sold mixtures suitable for making a porcelain body before 1796, when the patent expired, but several nineteenth-century ceramic writers say that they sold 'composition', a mixture which formed a glaze when fired. These two mills were nominally owned by individual members of the New Hall Company; in 1806, however, the Company itself enlarged its estate by buying some adjacent land and water. On this they built a mill and gained independence. Here steam power was used, for the 1831 New Hall Sale Advertisement mentioned 'the steam engine mill at Booden Brook'.

In spite of the difficult trading conditions of 1783 the first products of the factory were excellent and undoubtedly found a market. A large variety of wares were made which were decorated with restrained gilt decoration for 'Sunday best', as well as attractive, neat polychrome patterns. An invoice from New Hall to Josiah Wedgwood gives an idea of the contemporary prices and the relative importance of the different styles of decoration:

'Josiah Wedgwood Esq.,   Sept 7th 1789
Bt. of Hollins Warburton & Co.,
Manufacturers of Real China, Shelton,
                        Staffordshire.

1 Sett (sic) Cups and Saucers Enameld (sic)		
of 6 diffr^t Cups and 6 saucers	6	0
4 Cups & 4 Saucers Blue & White of 4 diffr^r		
patterns	3	6
1 Cup & Saucer White & Gold	2	5
	£0 11	11
Discount 25 pr Ct	3	0
	£0 8	11 '

This invoice shows that one cup and saucer cost $10\frac{1}{2}$d. if the decoration was blue-and-white, but 1s. when enamelled and 2s. 5d. gilded.

About this time the wide range of products was rationalised and soon a standard range of tea-sets was sold. The quality of decoration also became generally more pedestrian. The release in 1790 of their chief decorator, Duvivier, is clearly related to this change of policy (see page 58).

Nevertheless, although the wares were of a mundane quality they found a ready market. The paste and glaze were consistent and gradually improved so that the potting and translucency reached a good standard. Gas bubbles always filled the glaze but the pools of surplus glaze became shallower.

The style of decoration changed and—some think—deteriorated. No doubt it reflected contemporary taste and fashion. Tea-bowls gave way to handled teacups for this reason.

Partnership changes began in the nineteenth century. An announcement in the *Staffordshire Advertiser* of 10th November 1804 indicated that the original contract had expired:

'NOTICE

The Partnership term lately subsisting of and in the New Hall China Manufactory, at Shelton, in the parish of Stoke upon Trent, in the county of Stafford, having expired, the said Manufactory is now carried on at New Hall aforesaid, by Messrs. HOLLINS, WARBURTON, DANIEL, BAGNALL and CLOWES, only.
Shelton 8th Nov. 1804.'

These five names soon changed; Charles Bagnall retired and Jacob Warburton was replaced by his son Peter. The exact date of these changes is uncertain but it was before 26th April 1810, when the estate and all the buildings were purchased by Samuel Hollins of Shelton, Peter Warburton of Cobridge, John Daniel of Hanley, and William Clowes of Porthill for £6,800.

This important act showed courage and confidence. Economically the country was suffering the strain of war, whilst in the Potteries several firms like Davenport, Minton and Spode were developing confidently. However, the partners were obviously not concerned merely with their pots, they also had ideas for developing the land. The building of the Hope Congregational Church in 1812 on land next door to the factory is perhaps an indication of this, whilst the advertisement in the *Staffordshire Advertiser* in 1831, which announced the first attempt to sell the New Hall estate, is clear evidence of it (see page 24). Parcels of land were included in the offer.

The rise of other porcelain makers stimulated New Hall to maintain their standards and also to move with the times. The white bone-china body established by Spode was used by other potters and must have made the hard-paste porcelain seem dull and lifeless by comparison. Although New Hall were forced no doubt to abandon the hard-paste they had pioneered, they achieved the changeover without either apparent deterioration in standard of product or loss of sales momentum. The date for this changeover was probably between 1812 and 1814.

The events of the next few years were critical to the New Hall Company: the decline and fall was, I believe, inevitable.

If one looks at the names of the successful pottery and porcelain manufacturers it will be seen that they all have a consecutive tradition of individual leadership. Many, like Wedgwood, are from successive generations of one family. New Hall failed in this respect.

A joint stock company always has difficulty when a member dies. Unless a relative can carry on, either the remaining partners or an outsider must find the money to buy the vacant share. In the latter case a real leader seems unlikely to appear; such a man would surely venture on his own.

Two of the original partners had a son, but only one of these boys came into the business and showed the promise which could have led New Hall into the future. Peter Warburton, Jacob's son, was clever. In 1810 he perfected a new method of gold printed decoration and took out a patent for the process. About this time also he became a partner in place of his father, who obviously wished to retire. It was a tragedy that Peter Warburton died in 1813, predeceasing his father by thirteen years. This, I believe, was the knell of doom for New Hall.

All the original partners were near the end of their lives and although they must have been replaced at some time we have a record only of John Tittensor, who succeeded John Daniel as the manager in 1821. Tittensor had been a partner in a small Hanley potworks for a short time (1803–07) before joining New Hall as a traveller in 1815. The testimony to his success was his appointment as manager, a position which he held until the factory's end in 1835.

Despite these changes, many of the bone-china products are of excellent quality; evidently the factory was able to maintain its standards and withstand competition. Its name was respected since in 1830 (6th March) the name 'Hollins, Warburton, Daniel and Company' was amongst those appended to a petition denouncing 'truck' published in the *Staffordshire Advertiser*. The signatories proudly claimed that they paid their wages in money and not in the bills of credit which could be redeemed only in certain shops, usually connected with the owner of the potbank. This was an insidious way of achieving a double profit.

The end of New Hall was now in sight. On Saturday, 5th March 1831, the following advertisement appeared in the *Staffordshire Advertiser*:

'STAFFORDSHIRE POTTERIES.

EXTENSIVE CHINA-WORKS, STEAM ENGINE, FLINT MILL
AND VALUABLE LAND FOR BUILDING PURPOSES.
   TO BE SOLD BY AUCTION,
      BY MR. R. JOHNSON.

At the Swan Inn, in HANLEY, *in the county of Stafford, on Thursday the 24th day of March, 1831, at four o'clock in the afternoon, either altogether or in the following lots, namely:*

LOT 1. ALL that long established CHINA WORK, called the NEW HALL, situate in SHELTON, in the Staffordshire Potteries, comprising the Warehouses and plot of Land fronting to New Hall Street, and the Dwelling-house adjoining, in the occupation of Mr. John Tittensor, together with the Workshops, Buildings and Yards, and every requisite convenience for carrying on a most extensive business, the whole including an area, of about 7,200 superficial yards.

This lot is bounded on the south side by New Hall Street, and on the west by Brook Street, and has a communication with Hope Street on the east. In addition to its great extent, from its central situation on the main line of thoroughfare through the Potteries, it possesses local advantages for business, which can scarcely be equalled.

LOT 2—All that STEAM ENGINE MILL, with the valuable machinery and apparatus belonging thereto, used for the grinding of flint and potter's materials, situate at Booden Brook, in Shelton aforesaid, and in the holding of Mr. Thomas Crockett, together with the dwelling-house, garden and yard adjoining, the whole containing about 6,715 superficial yards of Land.

LOT 3—The several pieces or parcels of Land lying between Great York Street, and Booden Brook and Brook Street aforesaid, and on the east side of Great York Street, contiguous to lot 1, and also on the east side of Hope Street, fronting to certain New Streets already marked or laid out, and named *Peers Street, Union Street, Cross Street, Trafalgar Row, Paddock Street,* and *Brian's Wood Street*: the whole comprising 13A. 1R. 3p. of LAND, presenting a variety of the most eligible situations for building purposes.

Also, sundry BUILDINGS, consisting of a Dwelling-House, Barn, Stable and Hovel, with the Yard about the same, situate on the

C. Three teapots decorated in enamels (pattern 20). New Hall, hard-paste, c. 1782–7; teapot (right) ht. 6¼ in. See pages 35 and 36

south west side of Brook Street, and containing about 448 superficial yards, which will form part of lot 3.

The above property is all copyhold of inheritance of the manor of
Newcastle-under-Lyme.

A plan of the premises, shewing the boundaries of the several
pieces of Land comprised in lot 3, and the lines of the different
streets intersecting the same, may be seen on application to
MR. JOHN TITTENSOR, at the New Hall Manufactory, who will
attend with parties upon the premises.

Further information may be obtained of Mr. LEWIS GEORGE
HALES, Land Surveyor, Cobridge, or at the office of Messrs.
TOMLINSON, Solicitors, Cliff-Ville.

2nd March, 1831.'

It would seem that there were no buyers since in the following
year the *Staffordshire Advertiser* of 25th August and 1st September
had this advertisement:

'TO BE LET.

THAT old-established CHINA MANUFACTORY, called the NEW HALL,
situate in Shelton, with or without about fourteen acres of Land.
The premises are in an excellent situation, and of considerable
magnitude, and capable of doing an extensive business. Possession
to be given at the convenience of the coming-in Tenant.—For
particulars, apply to MR. JOHN TITTENSOR, on the Premises.'

R. G. Haggar, the eminent Staffordshire ceramic historian, has
suggested the possibility that Francis and Nicholas Dillon, earthenware manufacturers, were involved in the New Hall affairs and
possibly had control of the works.[1] This would explain why an
announcement in the *Staffordshire Advertiser* for 24th November
1832 asked for the creditors of the previous Dillon partnerships to
submit any outstanding accounts to John Tittensor at the New Hall
Works for scrutiny.

Trade was not very good at this time and there was considerable
unrest among the labour force. They had been beaten when they
struck in 1825 but now Robert Owen, the socialist, was preaching
about the success achieved elsewhere. A new trade union (the first
was in 1824) was formed and a strike in 1834 was successful. It is
unlikely that the New Hall factory, having been for sale in 1831, and
to be let in 1832, even attempted to cope with these conditions and

[1] *Apollo*, 1951, p. 133.

the announcement of 5th September 1835 in the *Staffordshire Advertiser* comes as no surprise:

'NEW HALL MANUFACTORY, SHELTON, POTTERIES.

EXTENSIVE SALE OF VALUABLE CHINA.

DEALERS and others are respectfully informed, that MR. MAIN-WARING is instructed to Sell the whole of this superb, useful, and valuable STOCK,

BY AUCTION, without reserve;

The Company of Proprietors having concluded on retiring from trade.

Further particulars will appear in future advertisements and handbills.'

Three weeks later, on 26th September, a more detailed advertisement appeared:

'NEW HALL CHINA MANUFACTORY, SHELTON.

VALUABLE & EXTENSIVE STOCK OF BURNISHED
GOLD CHINA.
TO BE SOLD BY AUCTION,
BY MR. JOHNSON,

On the premises, at the New Hall China Manufactory, at Shelton, in the Staffordshire Potteries, on Monday, Tuesday, Wednesday, Thursday, and Friday, the 5th, 6th, 7th, 8th, and 9th days of October, 1835, and the following week, (if necessary);

ALL the very valuable Stock of Burnished Gold and other CHINA, which consists of complete rich burnished gold tea services, in a great variety of shapes and patterns; also breakfast services to correspond. A very choice assortment of dessert and toilet services, with numerous modern and fancy-shaped jugs and mugs, chimney ornaments, &c. &c. A very general assortment of Common, China, Hawkers' Sets, &c.

This will be found a most advantageous opportunity for Merchants and China Dealers, who may rely upon every liberality being exercised towards their interest as purchasers to sell again. Likewise Inn-Keepers and the public in general, who are desirous of supplying themselves with a small assortment for their own use will find this Sale well deserving their attention.

The New Hall Company are declining business, and have let the premises, which they now occupy, with immediate possession; a circumstance which makes it quite necessary that they should dispose of their Stock without reserve.

The sale will commence each morning at eleven o'clock.'

THE NEW HALL CHINA MANUFACTORY 1781–1835

Thus the New Hall China Manufactory, which opened as a brave venture in 1781, closed without acclaim in 1835. Some of their products can be compared with the best porcelain from other factories but much was quite ordinary. The changes in shape and decoration reflect the changes in contemporary public taste and habit. A comprehensive collection of New Hall porcelain is not merely a record of the output of this small group of Staffordshire potters, it is also a social document, a vignette in which may be seen the changing aesthetic taste of the new industrial society.

4

THE PASTE AND GLAZE

Did New Hall really make hard-paste porcelain? How often this question is asked. The simple answer is yes, but the explanation is more complicated.

Superficially there is no problem. It has been shown that New Hall bought Champion's patent rights and we know that they styled themselves 'Manufacturers of real porcelain' in some of their invoices, and yet the appearance of their porcelain is visibly different from the Chinese, Continental and Plymouth/Bristol products. However, this difference can be explained and does not invalidate the claim that New Hall made hard-paste porcelain.

Firstly, the terms soft- and hard-paste must be defined. Most definitions quote the raw material composition and include the process by which the ingredients were used. This latter point is, I believe, a side issue and is responsible for the confusion about the kind of porcelain which was made by the New Hall China Manufactory.

Fundamentally the difference between hard- and soft-paste porcelain lies in the materials which are mixed so that, when fired to a high enough temperature, a common clay is transmuted to a translucent porcelain. True or hard-paste porcelain was first made by the Chinese, and other countries tried to emulate their achievement. In England, William Cookworthy was the first to find growan- or china-stone (the Chinese called it petuntse) and when he was able to use it with china-clay (kaolin) to make porcelain he obtained patent protection. Until this patent expired all other English porcelain makers, unless working illegally or under licence, must have made what is called artificial or soft-paste porcelain. The early artificial or soft-paste porcelains which were made at Chelsea, Derby and Longton Hall had glass in their composition. Bow and Lowestoft added ox-bone ash. At Worcester and Caughley steatite or soapstone was used instead of the clay (this is not as dramatic a difference as it sounds. China-clay is potassium aluminium silicate and soapstone is magnesium aluminium silicate).

28

These artificial bodies, especially those made at Bow, Chelsea and Derby, are physically softer than the Chinese porcelain and thus the term soft-paste is used.[1]

It seems to be a natural consequence for collectors to attempt to distinguish between the two kinds of porcelain by using a file on the footrim of the piece. This practice can only be deprecated; not only can the answer be misleading but the test piece is defaced. The physical hardness of the piece can depend upon the temperature at which it was formed as well as upon its composition. Some parts of an oven could produce better results than others: there was skill in placing the saggers[2] in a kiln.

Although close and careful examination of a piece can give some clue to its composition, the only certain way in which hard- and soft-paste can be differentiated is by chemical analysis. Even here there are problems and the interpretation of the results must be done carefully. G. E. Stringer quotes two analyses: one done by Eccles and Rackham in 1922, and one which he had done by Dr. H. W. Webb. In discussing these analyses Mr. Stringer only compares them together whereas they must be considered alongside the analyses of glassy, soapstone and china-stone bodies. From the figures quoted in the Table on page 30 it is obvious that the alumina and silica content of the Chinese and Bristol hard-paste bodies are very similar and quite different from those of other factories. The two New Hall analyses show clearly that their body is hard-paste.

Soft-paste porcelain was made in two distinct firing stages. In the first, the biscuit stage, the shaped clay was fired at about 1,100°–1,200°C, when it became translucent. Then this biscuit, as it is called, after being dipped in glaze, was fired again at about 900°C. This sequence of biscuit higher fired than glaze was natural to English potters and had been used for the making of Staffordshire earthenware at least since lead glaze replaced salt glaze. On the other hand, Chinese porcelain was made by a different firing sequence. The first firing was at about 900°C, after which the body had completely dried out and lost some water of reaction from the ingredients. However, true fusion had not begun. This body, which was firm enough to handle safely but would not withstand rough usage, was then dipped in glaze before being given its real firing at 1,300°–1,400°C. It was during this stage that the body achieved its translucency and, since the glaze matured simultaneously it fused into the under-body. This

---

[1] Soft-paste is actually a translation of the French *pâte tendre*.

[2] A sagger is a protective box made from fired clay in which the newly-made articles were placed for firing. It protected these articles from excessive local fierceness of the fire.

FACTORY	CHELSEA	LONGTON HALL	BOW	LOWESTOFT	DERBY	WORCESTER	CAUGHLEY	CHINESE	BRISTOL H P	NEW HALL	NEW HALL*	CHAMBERLAIN
Silica	64·76	76·16	43·58	41·42	41·94	72·80	74·22	71·82	69·96	73·56	68·37	75·36
Alumina	6·00	4·30	8·36	9·62	15·97	6·90	8·50	25·04	24·43	19·30	23·54	18·87
Lime	25·00	9·28	24·47	25·40	24·28	4·00	2·78	0·63	1·50	4·02	1·16	2·81
Phosphoric Acid	0·23	nil	18·95	18·77	14·96	—						
Magnesia	trace	nil	0·60	—	0·20	11·85	7·62	trace	trace	trace	0·22	0·18
Potash	2·58	—	0·85	—	0·90	—	1·28	1·89	1·36	2·10	3·42	1·27
Soda	1·82	—	1·20	—	1·06	—	2·27	2·12	1·92	0·92	1·16	2·00
Lead oxide	0·55	6·50	1·75	—	0·36	—	3·73	0·60	1·50	0·67	0·43	—
Total	100·94	96·24	99·76	95·21	99·67	95·55	100·60	100·29	100·84	100·81	98·70	100·65

RESULTS OF THE ANALYSIS OF PORCELAIN SPECIMENS MADE BY DIFFERENT FACTORIES

Reproduced from *Analysed Specimens of English Porcelain* by H. Eccles and H. Rackham, 1922, by courtesy of the Victoria and Albert Museum.

* This analysis was carried out for G. E. Stringer and quoted in his book *New Hall Porcelain*.

sequence of firing was used for making hard-paste porcelain by Cook-worthy at Plymouth and by Champion at Bristol, which suggests how the definition embracing both process and materials developed. But it need not always be so and New Hall was the first factory to combine the hard-paste materials by the more English firing sequence of high temperature biscuit followed by lower temperature glaze. This achievement was a major breakthrough in porcelain manufacture, though we do not know who made it. Was this Champion's final success or was it the first achievement of the Staffordshire potters? I favour the latter view but there is no evidence. There is evidence, however, that hard-paste porcelain can be made by this process for unglazed pieces of hard-paste biscuit porcelain have been dug up on the site of the old Caughley factory.

The principal differences between Bristol and New Hall porcelain lay in the process by which they were made, and in the glaze. The original Bristol glaze had to be modified so that it could be formed at a lower temperature and this was probably done by adding fluxes. Certainly lead was used, for the 100 New Hall pieces which I have tested all contained a good proportion of lead. I have not, however, found lead in any Bristol glazes that I have tested. In the beginning this new glaze had poor flow properties and often lay thickly on a piece. On the bottom of early teapots you see streaks in the glaze as though some excess glaze has been wiped away by drawing the fingers across. On tea-caddies and round teapots the glaze often failed to flow out completely and there are patches of raw paste to be seen near the base. When saucers and bowls were stood upside down for the glaze to drain and dry, small pools of glaze accumulated around the rim. This is often a good aid to recognition. Many eighteenth-century glazes frothed and bubbled when being formed (carbon dioxide is released when the materials interact) and the New Hall glaze always shows a mass of gas bubbles in it, especially in the thick areas in the footrims and where handle and spout join the body. These probably account for the relatively low gloss of the glaze since the surface is frequently covered with minute burst bubbles. New Hall imitators can often be spotted by their glaze being too shiny.

The presence of wreathing, or diagonal marks, on the sides of tea-pots, jugs and bowls is often said to be a characteristic of Plymouth and Bristol porcelains. It is found on some New Hall wares and also on pieces made by other factories. I believe that it is a mechanical property of the ingredients and is, therefore, likely to be found on pieces of porcelain made by any factory which used a mixture of china-clay and -stone.

The benefits which came from the improved manufacturing

technique were manifold. The firing sequence was the same one with which these Staffordshire potters were familiar and the lower firing temperature was more economical in fuel. The higher Bristol firing temperature must have been difficult to maintain and control and their kiln losses were notoriously high. It is no wonder that from the outset New Hall made a good, consistent product. Above all, they were able to make underglaze transfer-printed blue-and-white wares. It has been said that if only Bristol had been able to make ordinary blue-and-white china readily they could have had a more stable financial background. They could not do so because the body, after the first firing, was not really hard enough to withstand the rigours of transfer-application. The New Hall biscuit was: furthermore, the lower glaze temperature used by New Hall enabled them to produce a more satisfactory and acceptable underglaze blue colour.

Hard-paste was made until some time after 1811. By then its production was well controlled. The body could be finely potted, and the glaze, which contained fewer gas bubbles than in the early years, fitted closely. It is a pity that the standard of decoration was not improved or even maintained. From the beginning of the nineteenth century other factories were making bone-china, a body which consisted of clay, stone and bone ash. The bone ash not only strengthened the body but gave it a very white translucent appearance, a fine foil for coloured enamel decoration. By comparison, New Hall's grey hard-paste must have looked rather dull, so that eventually they must have been forced to change over to the new bone-china formula.

Obviously the changeover was achieved without much difficulty, since the New Hall version was a good quality porcelain with a clean, clear glaze. Unfortunately for the collector, most bone-china has a similar appearance, and unless there is some identity mark or novel shape it is very difficult to distinguish one factory's products from another. In the first years at New Hall the glaze frequently exhibited black specks. Later on, the quality of the paste and glaze was as high as has ever been achieved.

The date of the change from hard-paste to bone-china can only be surmised, but there are facts from which to work. A New Hall invoice dated 1810 describes the factory as making 'real-china' and a hard-paste jug dated 1811 is known (Plate 152).

In 1810 Peter Warburton enrolled his patent for the application of gold transfer-prints to porcelain. The lowest known pattern using this process is number 846 (recorded on a hard-paste plate in the Victoria and Albert Museum. Plate 150). Further, pattern number 984 is commonly found on both hard-paste and bone-china bodies, and pattern number 1046 is the highest known on the hard-paste body alone. It would seem then that the bone-china body was introduced first when the pattern book was at about number 1000 and this would possibly be about 1814. The changeover could have occurred in any year after 1811 and most writers suggest 1812. But on the evidence of pattern numbers I think that it was closer to 1814.

5

THE WARES

Much porcelain is commonly described as 'New Hall' but by no means all of it was made at the New Hall China Manufactory. One of the reasons for the confusing similarities of style is that there was no patent protection for the shapes of wares or decoration during the period that New Hall porcelain was made; and the Staffordshire porcelain industry, which was expanding at the time, made many imitations. A detailed knowledge of the wares is necessary before one can recognize them and identify them accurately. The most important aids to recognition are details of shape because even when another factory copied a shape their moulds could not be exactly the same, and handles, spouts and knobs, for example, were not always put in exactly the same place.

The following outline of New Hall wares has been compiled by careful study of the different potting shapes and the patterns which were applied to them. Some patterns originally used during the hard-paste period were repeated on bone-china. Since some of these bone-china pieces bear a New Hall mark, we can be certain of the origin of the pattern and its associated number. The shapes of hard-paste services decorated with this pattern (accompanied by the appropriate number) can then be assigned to New Hall with confidence. The 'silver-shape' teapot in the Victoria and Albert Museum which has 'Ralph Clowes New Hall fecit' inscribed on the base (Plate 40) is a valuable piece of evidence regarding the origin of this particular shape. Many patterns and associated shapes of wares have been established by comparison with this teapot.

It is found that production during the hard-paste period falls roughly into three phases. At first the potters experimented, being prepared to make a wide range of products. During this period— 1781 to about 1787—many tea-sets included a tea-caddy and a spoon-tray, and the handles of the teapots, jugs and cups featured an over-lapping thumb-rest. The blue-and-white wares included leaf-shape pickle-trays, asparagus-shells and knife handles. Dessert-services were made. Then came a brief transitional period during which this diversity of ware was reduced and the shapes were modified and simplified, until after 1790 a standard, rather limited selection of services was retailed.

Teapots and Stands

The balance of evidence suggests that the globular teapot was the first type to be made and that it was shortly followed by the 'silver-shape' teapot, which will be discussed later.

Some of the globular teapots were hand thrown and are therefore found in a variety of shapes and sizes. This may be evidence that they were made first, for during the first few months of experimentation hand throwing might have been more likely than the use of moulds. Possibly, but by no means certainly, the earliest shape is the pot illustrated by Jewitt (Plate 1) and said to have been decorated by Duvivier. To my knowledge, no teapot with this body- and handle-shape has been positively identified as New Hall, although the teapot in the service illustrated in Plate 2 has many similar features. The only significant difference lies in the body moulding, which is more like corrugation than reeding. However, a careful examination does not reveal enough similarity in its paste and glaze for one to be absolutely certain of its origin. On the other hand, although the handles on the cream-jug and the coffee-cups in this service have individual characteristics, these features are found on pieces of undoubted New Hall manufacture (Plates 3, 4 and 5 (right)).

Another globular teapot, which may lay claim to having the earliest shape, has a handle of obvious Bristol influence (Colour Plate C). The shape and raised husk moulding is so similar to much Bristol porcelain that one is tempted to suggest it as a positive Bristol-New Hall link. But the dimensions do not agree with any Bristol handle I have seen and the crispness of the moulding and the number of husks is different.

The New Hall teapot whose shape is nearest to that in the Jewitt illustration has a very different handle.[1] This handle, which features a thumb-rest formed where two pieces of the handle overlap, is characteristic of early New Hall wares, being found on coffee-pots, teapots, jugs and coffee-cups. Clear scroll moulding at the overlap is often visible on teapots and coffee-pots, but on jugs and cups the thumb-rest is sometimes barely noticeable. The last recorded pattern number for a piece with this handle is 186, which suggests that it was a feature until about 1787. Thus these teapots and wares can perhaps be dated to the period 1781 to 1787, which was largely devoted to experimentation. I should point out here that although some large

[1] R. J. Charleston, *English Porcelain 1745–1850*, 1965, Plate 61a.

jugs of a later date are known with a modification of this handle, I do not consider that this disproves or contradicts the proposed dating.

The potters seem to have tried, without much success, to find an aesthetically pleasing shape for the globular teapot. To my mind only the smallest ones (Colour Plates C and E) and the faceted (Plate 26) and reeded ones can be spoken of in the same breath as those of more famous factories. The nearly round pots, both small and large, have rather stubby swan-neck spouts, definite footrims, and lids which sit on top of and overlap the neckband; but the rather ugly barrel-shaped pots (Plate 18) have a narrowing spout the upper line of which is nearly straight but whose lower line is a generous ogee curve. They have no footrims and their lids fit inside the neckbands. Both styles of teapot have the thumb-rest handle.

A globular teapot with a wide strap-like handle and backward pointing thumb-rest was made (Plate 18). Its footrim was shallow and its spout sometimes had a moulded chain of husks about an inch from the base, the lower half of which had ten facets. The lid is found usually resting on top of the neckband. Obviously the cross-section of these lids varies but the knobs start off with solid onion shape and later have the vent hole for the steam bored axially through them, a characteristic which was first conceived by New Hall designers and became almost a diagnostic feature of the later 'silver-shape' teapot. Very occasionally a flower knob is found (Colour Plate E).

Finally there are the rather attractive reeded and faceted (Plate 26) variants which usually have a pineapple- or pinecone-like knob. This different style of knob is found also with the reeded, faceted and fluted teapots in the later 'silver-shape' series. However, it is the handle of these pots which generates the most interest, for here we find the forerunner of the handles of the transitional and early experimental 'silver-shape' teapots. The terminals of the handle are arrow-shaped (whereas all previous and almost all of the post-1790 terminals are semicircles) and there is a most attractive and delicate narrowing of the strap as it nears the lower terminal. Altogether I find this faceted teapot the most satisfying.

The morphological development of the 'silver-shape' teapot, always spoken of as being typical of New Hall, can be traced in a most interesting manner. Evidence of the aptness of its name is found in silver teapots of this shape with contemporary hallmarks. These teapots have a straight tapering spout which is also found on the earliest porcelain examples. However, the silversmiths were not the originators of this spout; the Chinese featured it on their porcelain and the Staffordshire potters on their redwares and basaltes. On the other hand these early New Hall teapots did have one unusual feature (Plate 23) in that they rested upon four small rosettes, each with six petals around the central pistil. It has been suggested that these rosettes were to raise the pot from the table to prevent marking it, but they are not really big enough and besides, teapot-stands have been found *en suite*.

During the experimental and transitional phases the basic shape of the 'silver-shape' teapot remained static and the lid always fitted within a raised circular collar: it was the spout and handle which changed. The handle, which developed from the one on the faceted globular pot, is found now with a fine herring-bone moulding (Plate 27). As noted previously, the arrow-like terminals are quite characteristic of early teapots, though some specimens are found whose handle terminals are beautifully moulded like shells (Plate 27). The straight tapering spout always had oak leaf moulding on the underside and this was often attractively outlined with magenta or gold (Plate 23). When the spout changed to the more normal 'S' shape it still had leaf-moulding around the base and six shallow grooves running its full length. The final curved spout had facets on each side which were connected at the top and bottom by curved surfaces. There are a large number of different combinations of these features and the possibilities are multiplied by the appearance of reeded and faceted sides as well as various sizes of teapots. The lids, usually convex, went through a stage of being quite flat and, in the case of reeded and faceted specimens, had similar moulding. The knobs, as with those on the globular teapots, were initially solid and then flask-shape with the central vent hole: solid pine-cone knobs accompanied the faceted and reeded pots.

With few exceptions, the 'silver-shape' teapots described so far have been of a comparatively small size (base 5 in. by $4\frac{1}{4}$ in.), that is, smaller than most of the globular pots, and one of them is unusually small (base $4\frac{1}{2}$ in. by 4 in.). Considering their size, the obvious lines of development and the low numbers of the patterns found on them, we can be confident that they were products of the first period of New Hall production—the period of experiment and development between 1781 and 1787. At the end of this period came the larger transitional teapots which were made before production settled down to the standard plain 'silver-shape' with a smooth ear-shaped handle (pushed in rather than a full loop), no rosette feet, an S-curved spout and flask-shaped knob on the lid with its centrally-bored vent hole. There were three transitional variants with reeds (Colour Plate F), straight facets (Plate 56), and ogee-curved flutes (Plate 58) between the straight ridges found on all the other teapots. It is important in the case of the latter variant to remember that the straightness of these ridges was retained, for two of the New Hall imitators made teapots on which the line of the ridges followed the curves of the flutes (Plates 222 and 240). The lids of these teapots had shallow moulding matching that found on their sides and the knobs were usually solid pine-cones, the steam vent hole being through the top of the lid. The handles retained the herring-bone moulding of the earlier small prototypes but the ends of the handles were not always arrow-shaped. They became rounded and the handle itself lost the pronounced narrowing previously noted.

Although some of these transitional styles give a pleasant visual effect this is not always the case: it varied with the decoration and the way in which the lid and the collar sat on the body. No wonder the plain 'silver-shape' became standard. Its general appeal is reflected in the fact that it was made by New Hall until at least 1803 (there is a teapot in the Victoria and Albert Museum inscribed 'Sophia Sayer 1803') and that it was copied at other factories. The commonest patterns found on the transitional shapes are numbered between 150 and 210, which suggests that the transition period was between 1787 and 1789.

The globular teapots were the subject of experiment but never really became established and the 'silver-shape' teapot went through a series of interesting and often very attractive modifications before assuming the typical New Hall shape. This makes a neat story of the first eight years or so of the factory's life. On the other hand it seems likely that a new shape was introduced during these transitional years—the pot with an oval base and a waisted profile on which is superimposed curved fluting (Plate 39). Consideration of the date of this shape offers a timely reminder to the collector to exercise care when using pattern numbers as evidence for the dating of wares. Pattern 52, obviously first used in the opening years of the factory's life, has been recorded on a service featuring this shape. Careful consideration suggests that this is a case of an early pattern being re-issued on a later shape, because the glaze under the base of the teapot was well controlled and did not show the thick streaks so often found on the early 'silver-shape' teapots, and the cream-jug was the rather heavy, waisted, obconical shape featured in the transitional period. It would seem then that this shape was introduced at the end of the 1780's and was most popular during the 1790's, since the commonest patterns to appear on it are between numbers 250 and 350. New Hall was not the only factory to make this shape of teapot and examples are frequently found made by Barr or Chamberlain at Worcester and by Rose of Coalport when he was using the Caughley works after 1799.

Much of the excitement of collecting teapots is lost when the factory's production is established, for there are fewer interesting prototypes and modifications. Large oval-based teapots were introduced with either straight vertical sides (Plate 111) or gentle convex curved sides. On the straight vertical sided teapot the curved spout had an octagonal cross-section and the handle was a plain loop fitted on to the side of the pot in the same way as on the standard 'silver-shape' teapot, including the terminal shape. The handle shape and manner of attachment often help to distinguish it from teapots of similar shape made by the Caughley-Coalport, Minton, Spode, Miles Mason and Herculaneum factories. The lids fitted almost flush inside the very narrow retaining rim, and although the lid frequently had the under flange cut away to accommodate a small apron across the front of the opening of the teapot, it was not an invariable feature. The lids had a vent hole in front of the knob, which was of solid oval shape with a small pimple on the top. The spout of the convex sided pot had a smooth oval cross-section and was very much more bulbous where it joined the body than it was at the open end. The knob also was different (like the one on the sucrier, Plate 103). The wide range of patterns found on these two shapes suggests that they were introduced during the 1790's and were still made in the first decade of the nineteenth century.

As the eighteenth century drew to a close New Hall introduced a new shape of teapot which they made until the time came to change over from hard-paste to bone-china. Boat-shape (Plate 112) is the appropriate name given to this bulbous oval teapot, the collar of which rises up and flares out like a ship's prow. In the earlier specimens there is a balanced rhythm in the shape of the teapot which invites one to hold it and pour tea from it. In the later years the teapot grew in size so that although the line remained, the whole effect became rather ponderous (Plate 113). The plain loop handle started directly from the rim of the collar and had a slight but definite kick away from the body, which it joined above the footrim. The narrowing spout was of a definite triangular section and often had a knurled or thickened upper edge. The lid, which fitted well inside the collar, had no flange and was dome-like with a solid oval knob similar to that on the oval straight sided teapot. Some knobs were made to represent the fleur-de-lis (Plate 112). The colouring of the lily was in keeping with the decoration of the teapot.

A problem is set by the teapot whose handle had a strut between the body and the normal upper connecting point (Plate 141). It is most likely that it was a modification of the boat-shape teapot, although it is possible that it was a precursor of it, somewhere between the oval-

39

based convex sided pot (Plate 103 shows a sucrier of this shape) and the boat-shaped pot (Plate 112). It is not a very elegant style and when the decoration on it is uninspired it can be downright ugly; it is no wonder that not very many were made. The diagnostic features are the symmetrically curved collar inside which fits the rather high domed lid; the knob, which has a thick stem to attach it to the lid, and is a solid oval with a little pimple on top of it; and the spout, which has a similar cross-section to that of the boat-shaped teapot. The most important feature, however, is the handle, which apart from the small strut already mentioned has a forward pointing thumb-rest, a most unusual feature for a New Hall teapot handle.

The New Hall China Manufactory commenced with some interesting and attractive shapes and experimented in order to produce a popular range of wares; and yet, when they changed over to the bone-china body, they appear to have made only one shape of teapot, which was similar to that produced by almost all contemporary factories. This teapot had a rectangular base, lid-opening and lid, and its sides were characteristically bulbous with a definite concave section below the top flange in which sat the lid (Plate 179). The handle had a characteristic shape which represented a complete change from those we have seen already. On the other hand, the spout seems to have developed from that of the boat-shaped teapot. Only one size of teapot was normally made but I have seen a smaller teapot which appeared to have been made from a sucrier body on which a spout had replaced one of the handles!

The bone-china teapot was not an entirely new shape since an obvious forerunner was introduced at the end of the hard-paste period (Plate 50). Essentially it was the imposition of a rectangular ground-plan upon the boat-shaped teapot, and although it is usually found made of hard-paste, bone-china specimens occasionally turn up.

To a large extent the story of the teapot is the story of New Hall. Positive identification of its wares depends so much upon a knowledge of teapot shapes that it is very important to know the standard range. By linking the pieces in a service with a teapot of known shape an intelligible outline of the factory's production can be perceived, so that when an unusual piece is found, its date of production can often be ascertained by comparison with related standard pieces.

The teapot in every service had a stand but, although the simple shape of the stand makes it less susceptible to damage than the teapot, fewer seem to have withstood the passage of time. Quite naturally, they echoed the shape of the base of the teapot and if there is doubt about the provenance of a stand then its proportion and size can be

D. Tea-wares painted in enamels and gold. New Hall, hard-paste, c. 1782–95; spoon-tray, 1. 5¾ in., pattern 83; tea-caddy, ht. 5 in., pattern 89. See pages 45 and 49

used as evidence. The majority of New Hall teapot-stands had a flat unglazed base. In particular, this applied to the stands made for the 'silver-shape' and the straight sided and the ogee-waisted oval-based teapots (Plates 38, 111 and 86). When the 'silver-shape' teapot was reeded, faceted or fluted, this moulding was always followed by the side of the stand. Moulding enhanced their appearance and many of them are very attractive indeed.

The early round teapot-stand looked rather like a small plate and could on first acquaintance be taken for one. However, instead of the simple upward curve to the rim which is found on saucers and plates the shape was more sinuous and curved back to form a shallow everted rim.

A small footrim is found on the stands which accompany the boat-shaped and the oval-based, convex sided teapots. This must have improved the insulation between the hot teapot and the table and thus reduced the number of heat marks on table tops. Such footrims were usually shallow and formed by hollowing out the centre of the base. By this means the apparent outer edge of the footrim was actually a continuation of the side of the stand. Unlike the other teapot-stands they had the enclosed central part glazed.

The bone-china teapot-stand had a shallow footrim and was glazed underneath.

Coffee-Pots and Stands

The number of coffee-cups that can be found suggests that they were popular pieces and used widely. This is belied by the small number of coffee-pots that have survived, and the paltry number of different styles created. In fact, all the hard-paste coffee-pots had a similar silhouette (Plates 35 and 87). The early spouts were more like a swan's neck than the later ones, the typical thumb-rest handle preceded a plain loop and the line of the bulbous body became more ponderous as time went on. Reeded, faceted and spiral-fluted coffee-cups were made and so it seems likely that such moulding was used on the pots (Plate 52).

The bone-china coffee-pot (Plate 162) is of a completely different shape, clearly belonging to a different era. The illustrated example bears the concentric ring mark.

The stands for the coffee-pots resemble modern tea-plates. The footring has all the typical New Hall characteristics and the flange resembles a narrow, gently everted rim.

Jugs

Some of the most attractive and desirable pieces of porcelain made by any factory are cream-jugs and those made at New Hall, especially

41

in the early years, are no exception to this rule. Most can be classified readily and coupled with a related teapot shape, but occasionally an unusual specimen turns up to make the collector's life interesting and ensure that his collection is never complete.

Pear-shaped jugs, *en suite* with the various forms of globular teapot, were made and these are found with different spouts and handles. The combination of thumb-rest handle and spout with leaf-moulding beneath seems to be the most common (Plate 19) and sometimes this jug was covered.[1] Although the jug illustrated in this book is painted in coloured enamels it is more usual to find gilt decoration. A sparrow-beak spout and a flared pouring lip are known on jugs decorated with underglaze blue transfer-prints. The former with a small cover has a plain kinked loop handle (Plate 191) and the latter most frequently has a thumb-rest handle (Colour Plate E).

Two other styles of jug which were probably made to accompany a globular or barrel-shaped teapot may conveniently be mentioned here. The small round jug (Plate 21) with a small beak spout is one of the prettiest pieces I have seen. 'Robin jug' springs to mind as an apt description. It was thrown on the wheel and had either a plain handle or one with a thumb-rest. The other jug is of faceted sauceboat-shape (Plate 28).

The first common style was helmet-shaped and copied from silver. It was made to go with globular, early and transitional 'silver-shape' teapots. Three sizes were made (Plate 17), and these are found reeded and faceted as well as plain. The largest jugs usually went with the large 'silver-shape' teapot made during the transitional period but occasionally they are found with the smaller teapot (Plate 24). The plain jugs feature the thumb-rest handle which was noted on the globular teapot, and on the large plain jug there is an outward kink above the lower terminal (Plate 17). A forward pointing thumb-rest has been seen on a few of the large jugs instead of the customary overlapping thumb-rest but apparently this was not a standard feature. However, reeding (Plate 25) and faceting (Plate 31) on the body were considered to be sufficient embellishment and then invariably the handle is a plain loop.

The bodies of most of these jugs were almost round but some had pushed-in sides which appear almost triangular. With these the handle had an overlapping thumb-rest on the smaller size (Plate 55) and a plain loop on the larger size (Plate 47).

It was quite a natural development from these to the various forms of what has been called the obconical jug. These varied in size and, as with the helmet-shaped jug, were plain (Plate 83) and faceted

[1] R. J. Charleston, *op. cit.*, Plate 61a.

(Plate 51). In some cases, when a suitable decoration was applied, these jugs looked very neat and attractive but on other examples, for instance the waisted variant with curved fluting (Plate 60), the effect was ponderous. It is possible that the attempt to apply spiral fluting to the helmet jug led to the creation of the obconical jug which was introduced during the transitional period 1787–90. These jugs accompanied both 'silver-shape' and oval-based waisted teapots and were in production until almost the end of the century.

We are now at the stage when the jug bore a likeness to the teapot it accompanied. The smaller 'silver-shape' jug was quite charming and generally seemed to be decorated in a much neater manner than the run-of-the-mill larger one. I have not seen a faceted variant but there was a reeded one and there were two versions (Plates 64 and 73) with curved fluting: one of these retained the vertical ridges of the plain jug in the manner of the matching teapot. These jugs were designed to accompany the 'silver-shape' teapot but they were also to be found in services with the oval-based, waisted teapot.

An oval straight sided jug (Plate 114) went with the oval straight sided teapot and the sides had gentle convex curves when necessary (Plate 119). However, I have not seen a teapot matching the jug (Plate 118) in this series, which had curved fluting; the pattern number 480 dates it in the expected period of production (about 1795). These jugs had a shallow recess under the base which usually showed the characteristic New Hall bubbled glaze. The plain loop handle came from the back of the rim and rejoined the body about one inch above the base; and the concave neckband continued even under the handle, which usually distinguishes this New Hall jug from those made by the other factories using a similar style.

There were two jugs to match the boat-shape teapot. Predictably, the first one was the more elegant (Plate 81), matching the low, boat-shape pot. The later, larger and more bulbous version (Plate 123) was in keeping with the ornate gilt decoration which was usually applied to it: it was first made at the turn of the century. The handle on these jugs was a plain loop with a slight kick away from the body at its lower junction with it, but a jug with a forward-pointing thumb-rest on the top of the loop is recorded.[1] The latter jug probably accompanied the teapot with the strut handle, since this is the only teapot handle with a similar thumb-rest.

When the rectangular-plan teapot was introduced shortly before the change-over from the hard-paste to the bone-china body, it had a matching jug (Plate 157) which was not of a very elegant shape. It is a relief to find that the line was changed drastically when the standard

[1] T. A. Sprague, *Apollo*, Aug. 1950, Fig. VI.

bone-china shape was introduced. The jug was longer, with a smooth rim- and spout-line, and a clean handle shape with a small internal projecting cusp about one inch above the lower junction with the body. This shape was used with tea-services throughout the bone-china period (Plate 161).

Large jugs were made throughout the life of the factory, but they were never common or standard wares. One such jug was an adaptation of the first coffee-pot, on which the swan-neck spout had been replaced by a large beak-spout (Plate 20): it was probably made to meet a special order.

The most distinctive group of hard-paste jugs had a modification of the early thumb-rest handle; the lower section had an overlapping scroll by which device it changed its shape from a concave to a convex curve, ending in a free outward-pointing cusp (it should be noted particularly that the lower section overlaps outside the end of the upper section). Most of these jugs were made for presentation since they are extremely well decorated and often have added initials (Plates 13, 16 and Colour Plate A). A few were decorated with standard patterns and were marked with the relevant pattern number (Plate 66). These jugs were probably made from 1790 onwards.

The style of the larger jugs changed as the nineteenth century progressed and the shape used with the bone-china paste seems to be typical of the period (Plate 153). An important hard-paste jug of an intermediate shape must be mentioned here (Plate 152). Bearing the inscription 'John Brown, Yoxall, 1811' it provides good evidence that in this year New Hall were still making the hard-paste body.

Bas-relief is not commonly applied to bone-china; it goes more suitably on stoneware, in which medium John Turner, Adams, Davenport and Wedgwood specialized. Nevertheless, New Hall made a bone-china jug (Plate 182) decorated with a bas-relief of a hunting scene, which was painted out in lavender underneath the glaze. The underside of the spout and the handle were moulded. Other jugs were made (Plate 181) decorated with a relief-moulded hunting scene but they are not, in my opinion, a credit to the New Hall China Manufactory.

Sugar-Pots

Sugar-pots are amongst the most charming and distinctive pieces in the eighteenth-century tea-set. The occurrence of them in New Hall services, however, poses some interesting questions which are perhaps more in the field of the economist or sociologist than of the ceramist. Some tea-sets contained a covered sugar-pot, others an open sugar-basin. The tea-sets made during the experimental and transitional periods included covered pots, usually when the decoration was gilt, but the standard services with the 'silver-shape' teapot had an open basin, and these sets were most frequently decorated with polychrome sprig patterns. Furthermore, in the late hard-paste and the bone-china periods, nearly all tea-services had a covered sugar-pot and once more the decoration was mostly an ornate gilt pattern.

Why, in some services, were sugar-pots covered and in others left open? Was it simply because a 'silver-shape' sucrier had no aesthetic appeal or did the social habit of using sugar change? Can significance be attached to the appearance of the covered sugar-pot with gilded patterns and the open basin with a floral sprig pattern? It is probable that gilded wares were for 'Sunday best'. I offer no solution but the question is intriguing.

The covered sucriers of the early services were simple, round and without handles (Plate 49). They had the same shape of knob on the domed lid as was used on the teapot. These were onion- or flask-shaped on plain sucriers and pinecone-shaped on the sugar-pots which were reeded (Plate 37), faceted (Plate 24) or covered with curved flutes (Plate 59). Usually they were of a standard size, but smaller ones are known. The reeded, faceted and fluted sugar-pots were made to accompany the large transitional period 'silver-shape' teapots.

A feature of the next group of covered sugar-pots was the mock ring handles placed at each end. As was pointed out by Dr. T. A. Sprague[1] these rings were never completely attached to the body; the rings were made separately and then attached to the body at the top and bottom. It is an important diagnostic point, since almost all other factories included the rings as a part of the body moulding.

Three styles of oval-based sucriers are known. The waisted type (Plate 89) matched the teapot in many of its features, the comparatively deep footrim with the deep groove close to where it joins the body, the shape of the flanged lid which slightly overlapped the edge of the body, and the knob on it. Reeded (Colour Plate D) and spiral-fluted (Plate 60) variants are known and it is probable that the factory made one with facets.

Both the straight sided sucrier and the one with convex sides (Plate 103) matched the shape of the teapot in the set. The lid fitted on a narrow recessed rim and the knob was *en suite*.

Sucriers of two shapes went with the boat-shape teapots. Both have an oval base with a moderately shallow footrim, and the rather high domed lid fits inside the collar band, resting on a small rim. The difference between the two styles is that one has two small plain ear-like loop handles (Plate 142) (they are shorter and less generous than

[1] T. A. Sprague, *Apollo*, Oct. 1950, p. 109.

those of other factories) whereas the neckband on the other sugar-pots rises up to a boat-like prow at both ends and these serve as handles (Plate 130). Modifications of these shapes include inward-pointing thumb-rests on the ear handles and, in the case of the double boat-shape sucrier, a fleur-de-lis knob, obviously going with the smaller boat-shape teapot with the same knob.

The shape of the last covered sugar-pots in the New Hall range is predictable. A rectangular base, convex bulbous body and a rect-angular domed lid, fitting inside an undulating collar on the hard-paste original, but resting on a shallow rim set in the flat horizontal shoulder on the standard bone-paste sucrier. The handles in both cases have a shape similar to that used for the teapots.

Tea-bowls, Teacups, Saucers, Slop-Bowls, Plates, Coffee-Cups, Coffee-Cans

The identification of a single small piece of a service, like a tea-bowl or saucer, is usually difficult unless you have good experience of the characteristics of the paste and glaze of many different factories. There are few distinctive features to the simple New Hall wares nor is it possible to present a coherent story of developing style.

Tea-bowls varied widely in size but a common feature of the first period was an everted rim which can be easily detected by touch. The footrim was usually vertical sided with a rounding of the edges of the bottom rim. The most distinctive feature seems to be the glaze, which generally contains numerous gas bubbles, very noticeable wherever the glaze gathers in pools. These are found in curtain-like sections round the rim of the bowl (suggesting that the wares were placed face downward to drain after being dipped in glaze) and on the inside junction of the footrim and the base. On the other hand all traces of glaze were carefully cleaned from the bottom edge of the footrim, that is, the part on which it normally stands. It is very rare indeed to find any trace of glaze on this particular part of hard-paste New Hall wares and one should always suspect a piece with a glazed rim bottom as belonging to another factory. Tea-bowls were made and sold by New Hall until almost the end of the hard-paste period although cups with plain loop handles (Plate 138) were probably intro-duced about 1795 as an alternative: they had a very shallow, glazed, recessed base. Before the end of the hard-paste period an inner finger-ring was added to the handle (Plate 138) and this style was then continued in the bone-china period, during which time the ring was compressed and became an oval (Plate 154). The final cup shape with a 'Grecian handle' was typical of the 1820 period (Plate 172) being used by several contemporary factories. Occasionally large breakfast-cups are seen. These occur in both hard-paste and bone-china but otherwise have the same outline shape and handle as the teacups.

Since reeded, faceted and curved fluted ornament was applied to teapots, jugs and sugar-pots during the first and transitional periods the tea-bowls, saucers, coffee-cups, plates and slop-bowls were also made in these styles. The noteworthy points here are that the tea-bowls and coffee-cups had 28 reeds, 16 facets or 20 curved flutes and the saucers had the same number of reeds and facets but in the case of the curved flutes there were 24. The rarely found reeded cup and saucer which is slightly waisted has only 27 reeds.[1] Other points worth making in connection with the curved fluting are that it always appeared to have been spaciously conceived and never looked tight or cramped as was the case with the wares of other factories, and the spines or ribs which separated the flutes were not sharply raised. Since the moulding was shallow, the rims of cups and bowls showed little sign of it. It is not really surprising since drinking from a bowl or cup with a pronounced moulding on it would be rather uncomfortable.

The first coffee-cups had the overlapping thumb-rest handle and although there were a few attempts to imitate these they can usually be recognized as such. The shape and size of the cups varied widely so that it is impossible to classify them, but careful examination of the glaze will always confirm their origin. For a very short time, before a plain loop handle was introduced, coffee-cups had grooved handles similar to those used by many other contemporary factories (Plate 185).

In the second half of the 1780's plain loop handles were introduced and the shapes of the cups became more consistent; as with the tea-bowls, the everted rim was often in evidence. Reeded, faceted and curved-fluted variants were made though, as on the more important pieces, the handles were plain. In fact they were usually strap-like and frequently had pointed terminals similar to those found on some of the early teapots and jugs. The manner in which a handle was attached to the body of a cup is worthy of careful study as also is the shape of the terminals.[2]

About the same time as teacups appeared, New Hall changed from making coffee-cups to making coffee-cans. They usually had a very slight convex curve to their sides and a plain handle, but when finger-

---

[1] The difference in the number of curved flutes on bowls and saucers was first pointed out by Dr. Sprague in *Apollo*, Aug. 1950, p. 52.

[2] As a general rule New Hall applied handles only of the shapes described above. However, a few examples of cups whose kinked handle resembles that made later by Spode and other manufacturers, have been noted (Plate 54). For a very short time, about 1790, New Hall made teacups with this handle as an alternative to tea-bowls.

loops were introduced to teacup handles, so they were to coffee-cans. During the bone-china period the coffee-cups were similar in shape and style of handle to the teacups: they were very dainty (Colour Plate H).

The diameter and depth of the saucers varied considerably and generalization is difficult. However, in the hard-paste period the foot-rim matched that of the tea-bowl in cross-section, lack of glaze on the actual ring and accumulation of bubbled glaze within the footrim and in curtains round the outside top edge of the saucer. Moulded saucers are very attractive and are keenly sought after. In general, the sharpness and depth of fluting and reeding is markedly less on New Hall wares than on those of other factories. It is specially the case with the faceted and fluted saucers where the moulding soon merges into a smooth surface. Painting decoration on these saucers must have been much easier than on the partnering cups and bowls. At no time during New Hall's life was a well for the cup made in the bottom of the saucer. Originally this was probably because tea was poured from the tea-bowl into the saucer before it was drunk. The centre of the saucer inside was flat and the sharpness of the upward curve to the rim depended on the depth of the saucer. During the bone-paste period, however, the saucers became deeper and had straight, angled sides from the centre flat area. This shape matched that of the cups admirably.

Slop-bowls were of a remarkably consistent shape and size throughout the hard-paste period. The footrims were quite deep, especially in the first decade, but they were generally larger versions of the tea-bowl footrim, a parallel-sided, rounded footring without any glaze on it and pools of bubbled glaze in the footrim junction with the base. The number of reeds, facets and curved flutes was the same as was used on the tea-bowl. However, there were two profiles in the bone-paste period. One was similar to the hard-paste bowl but with a round footrim (Plate 173) and the other had angular sides which matched the outline of the cups (Plate 160).

Bread-plates, throughout the factory's life, were generally without a flange. Like the saucers they were flat with upward curved rims. In fact they are usually called saucer-dishes. In the early years the plates were shallow and the upward curve was gentle, but as time went by the curve became more pronounced at the edge although the depth did not increase very much. Early plates often showed signs of sagging within the footrim, an observation which calls to mind the difficulty which Champion had at Bristol when making flat ware and how he sometimes used an extra support as the remedy.

The occurrence of a few flanged plates creates a problem. In bone-china they were made for dessert-services (Plate 171) but the use of the hard-paste plates (usually smaller than a normal saucer-dish) is obscure.

Miscellaneous Ware

Tea- and coffee-services were the staple productions of the New Hall China Manufactory and all representative collections of the factory's ware are built around their developing shapes. It follows that the collector finds interesting, and in many cases rare, pieces to enlarge his collection wherever the makers digressed from their main purpose. The kind of piece made of hard-paste porcelain is so different from that made of bone-china that it is more convenient to consider the two groups separately.

Many of the rare and unusual hard-paste pieces were made during the first decade. This was when the manufacturers seem to have been most swayed by ambition and when experiment abounded.

Many tea-services were completed with a tea-caddy and a spoon-tray, just as they were when made at Worcester, Caughley and Derby. At New Hall most of these full services were decorated with gilt patterns and only a few bore the simple polychrome sprigs or under-glaze blue transfers. The style of decoration found on these services must have been dictated by the public. In the last two decades of the eighteenth century it is probable that blue-and-white decoration and coloured enamels were used on everyday wares but gilt decoration was demanded for the 'Sunday best' services.

Even in 1780 tea was a special drink and expensive. The lady of the house took great care of it and often kept it under lock and key. Certainly servants were not always trusted with its care. Thus it was natural for a best porcelain tea-set to have its own caddy. Quite a number have survived but relatively few of these still have a lid.

The first tea-caddies were hand thrown and each had an individual jar shape. Their domed lid overlapped the caddy's neck and had a plain knob (Plate 10). This knob is so small that it slips easily from the grasp; it is little wonder that few have survived. Surely the highest mortality rate in porcelain affects the tea-caddy lid.

Reeded and faceted tea-sets were made and so we find tea-caddies *en suite* (Plates 11 and 24). By contrast with the plain ones, these had no neckband and their lid, which usually had a small pine-cone knob, fitted flush into the shoulder. These cone knobs were even harder to grasp than the plain ones and they were sometimes replaced by a plain knob (Colour Plate D).

E

The last shape of caddy (Plate 79) matched the 'silver-shape' teapot, but few are seen. The probable reason for this is that the introduction of the 'silver-shape' heralded the end of the factory's experimental period and the beginning of the marketing of standard sets in which fancy extras were no longer included.

Spoon-trays are extremely rare either because fewer were made than even tea-caddies or, more likely, because they were useful as pin-trays when the tea-service was cast aside. The suggestion that they could be used for pins lays emphasis on their size. They were small (about $5\frac{3}{4}$ inches long) and were originally made for holding tea-spoons so that the saucer was free to be used for tea drinking or, perhaps, because teaspoons were too long and heavy to be easily balanced in a saucer. Small teapot-stands should not be confused with spoon-trays. A dessertspoon or small tablespoon would be more suitable than a teaspoon for these! Two shapes of spoon-tray are known. One is of quatrefoil form and the other, like the product of other factories, of long hexagonal shape (Plate 12).

According to Jewitt,[1] both dinner- and dessert-services were made, but they are seldom found. The dessert-services featured fine mould-ing which formed the outline of shells. In some cases this moulding was filled with bright blue lines and the outline completed with gold. Alternatively, a very dark blue colour formed a border around the edge of the plate up to and around the moulded shells, which were then edged with gold. These must have made handsome but simple services centred upon lobed centre plates, some with pierced edges, stands and heart-shaped dishes (Plates 6 and 7).

Occasionally a flanged plate is found (Plate 135) decorated with a stock pattern and these possibly belonged to a dessert-service.

Accessories for the dinner table such as leaf-dishes (Plate 188) and asparagus-servers (Plate 186) occur only in blue-and-white. Similarly, knife handles (Plate 187) seem only to bear this type of decoration.

Moulded pieces occur as a minor part of the New Hall range. Like most other factories they made two sizes of cream-jugs which feature moulded leaves rising up from the base. The smaller size (Plate 3) seems to be the more elegant, but both are attractive and can be found decorated with early standard polychrome patterns as well as under-glaze blue transfer-prints (Plate 193). Their handles form their most important feature, with the thumb-rest piece at the top and the overlap piece in the middle. Usually there is leaf moulding between the body of the jug and the thumb-rest and on the larger jugs the upper handle joint is covered by a moulded shell.

Mugs were made in various sizes and although the later ones were

[1] Ll. Jewitt, *op. cit.*, vol. 2, p. 309.

quite plain (Plate 91) the early ones had overlapping leaf moulding on the body and a similar handle to the cream-jugs just mentioned.[1]

These particular handles would seem to be the link with that group of tea-wares which although of undoubted hard-paste and often decorated with standard New Hall patterns does not always show unmistakable characteristics of paste and glaze (Plates 2 and 5). The principle feature of this group, apart from the handle, is the moulding, which is more like corrugation than the commonly found reeding. These wares must have been made by New Hall during the first year or two of production.

Some large jugs (Plate 4) seem on the evidence of paste, glaze, handle and moulding to be products of this Staffordshire factory and they are very attractive pieces of porcelain. Since the specimens I know are dated and bear either a name or initials it is likely that they were made as presents or for presentation. Unfortunately their inscription weakens the case for their being New Hall jugs. The style and shape suggests that they were made in the first six or so years of production but the enamelled dates are 1790 and 1793. The enamelling is of very high quality but the palette and brightness of the colours are not typically New Hall's. In spite of this somewhat conflicting evidence it seems likely that they were made at New Hall but painted by an outside decorator.

Obviously the making of presentation pieces was part of the New Hall repertoire. Splendid jugs were made with a modification of the early thumb-rest handle, some dated, some with initials and others, most desirable of all, decorated by Duvivier. These bore fine decoration but there were others made for a more mundane world which were decorated with a standard pattern and were even marked with the relevant pattern number. I think that all these jugs were made after 1790.

Dated and presentation pieces can often be used as valuable evidence in creating a chronological picture of a factory's wares. Unfortunately some pieces turn up which either topple the castle or need a special explanation. An example of this is a globular teapot (Plate 57) which is inscribed 'Whether ye eat or drink or Whatsoever ye do, do all to the Glory of God. Johnathan and Betty Wood. 1798', in enamels. The inscription was painted at the same time as the rest of the decoration. The pattern number is written beneath the pot 'No 195' which suggests that the decoration was done at the factory. The apparent contradictions here are that the production of globular teapots is thought to be complete well before 1790 and at the time when globular teapots were made the pattern number was not put

[1] R. J. Charleston, *op. cit.*, Plate 63b.

on the piece. Furthermore, it is unusual for the lid on this shape of teapot to be within the neck opening; it usually sits on top of the neck. However, since the pot was thrown on a wheel it could presumably have been made at any time. Another teapot of this shape was illustrated by G. E. Stringer.[1] It also bore this verse inscription, which is a modification of 1 Corinthians X, 31, and the added names 'John and Mary Wood'. In this case the inscription was in gilding and need not have been done at the factory. It is rather a coincidence to find both these teapots bearing the same inscription and the name of a couple called Wood. A further coincidence is that a large jug of the form mentioned in the previous paragraph is inscribed in gold 'J. & E. Wood, Padiham 1800'.[2] I am sure that there is a direct connection between these three pieces and a likely explanation is that all three were made as wedding presents, for members of the Wood family of Padiham in Lancashire. I must admit, however, that a search of the Parish Registers, kindly carried out for me by the Rev. R. C. Hudson, has not revealed any evidence to support this theory.

Chocolate-cups (Plate 124), or perhaps they were caudle-cups or posset-pots, are uncommon. Although they were probably made to special order, they must have been generally available since they were decorated with standard patterns. The cups had a lid and stood on a saucer with a shallow well in the bottom. The specimens with the twisted leaf-stalk handles and knob (Plate 63) are earlier than those with the ring handles and simple gilt knob. Since these pieces were usually decorated with gilt patterns it is possible that some are lurking in cabinets containing Chamberlain's Worcester porcelain. On the other hand a fine open bowl (possibly for broth), with entwined twig handles, which is decorated in a typical sprig pattern is unmistakably New Hall (Plate 115).

The present section would be incomplete without mentioning punch-bowls. Large bowls in sizes up to fourteen inches in diameter were made. Eleven-inch bowls decorated with the window pattern (number 425) are seen quite often but not so those with earlier patterns (e.g. numbers 83 and 153). This size of bowl seems to be quite deep with rather upright sides but when the diameter was increased the sides flared outwards suggesting use as a punch-bowl rather than as a wash-basin. The decoration of these larger bowls was usually a combination of parts of several different standard patterns and thus they were not always numbered or marked.

Much of the interesting and unusual hard-paste porcelain was made during the first challenging years of experimentation. By the time

[1] G. E. Stringer, *op. cit.*, Plate XV.
[2] R. J. Charleston, *op. cit.*, Plate XII.

that the bone-china body had become established the factory's output was standardised and reduced to a single style of tea-service. The prospect offered to the collector is bleak. An interest can be maintained, however, since new shapes were occasionally introduced.

Dessert-services are most interesting. They have an embossed moulding of white flowers on a pale blue, pink (Plate 171) or green ground round the flange of the plate. The central decorative motif varied and was often strikingly attractive: a basket of fruit, a bouquet of flowers or the country house scenes applied to tea-services and given the pattern number 984. Interesting and attractively shaped dishes were made as well as the normal plates. Heart-shaped and waisted rectangular dishes (Plate 170) were the focus of the service and sauce- or custard-tureens (Plate 169) sometimes completed the set.

Covered cups and bowls (Plate 163) are always interesting though frequently the covers are either lost or broken. Chocolate- or caudle-cups (Plate 174) were made in bone-china using the same moulds as had been used with the earlier hard-paste body. On the other hand breakfast-sets are found only in bone-china. These sets contained attractive butter- and preserve-dishes which were sometimes attached to the base saucer like the dessert sauce-tureen. Unfortunately, the lids and covers are often missing (Colour Plate H).

The decorative jugs featuring horses in bas-relief have been mentioned already. They were probably part of a popular range since the sale notice of 1835 (p. 26) mentions 'modern and fancy-shaped jugs and mugs'. No chimney ornaments have yet been recorded, but the pair of ornate vases (Plate 183) could have been used on a side table. Here is an opportunity to enlarge the present field of knowledge.

6

DECORATION, DECORATORS
AND MARKS

DECORATION

The range of decoration used by New Hall is seldom appreciated. Originally collectors recognised only the coloured sprig patterns. Later came a knowledge of the use of underglaze blue transfers. A sparing use of gold was noticed especially as a rim or edge decoration. Finally came the realisation that gold was used in both simple and elaborate designs. In fact it is known now that gold was used more frequently than any colour even from the earliest days.

When looking at the sequence of patterns we can see how the public taste changed, or rather deteriorated. The first gilt patterns were discreet and elegant (patterns 52, 83, 89), frequently showing a Meissen influence (patterns 152–155) (Colour Plate F) and often a range of patterns produced by using a single basic device. One example of this latter is a narrow mazarine blue band under the glaze finished by innumerable different overglaze gold lines and motifs (Plates 8 and 9). Another range of patterns was produced with different coloured bands within two different styles of gilt border; patterns 167 (apricot) and 206 (yellow), for example, are different coloured bands within plain gold lines and these become pattern numbers 222 and 221 when black lines and a small gilt leaf border are added to the border. All these patterns were probably introduced before 1790.

Public taste changed as more families and a different class afforded a porcelain tea-set, and the style of decoration also changed. Gilt decoration tended to cover more of the porcelain surface instead of being restricted to a simple border. The gold appeared in greater evidence. Although some attractive borders were still made, e.g. gold foliage incorporating simple flowers (pattern 445—fuchsias) or berries (pattern 291—rose hips), the tendency was to cover much of the surface with an underglaze dark blue and to complete the pattern with designs in gold (patterns 581 and 779). The designer often let his imagination run amok, producing bunches of orange and blue grapes as well as natural yellow-green ones. Some of the animals used are grotesque, either intended to be like real animals, e.g. elephants and lions (patterns 1054 and 1214) which the decorator had probably never seen in real life, or else perhaps of heraldic or mythological origin (pattern 550).

In the bone-china period, gold was used with more discretion. Generally it would seem that its use was to complete a pattern rather than form a main part of it. The white body was seemingly more suited to bright colours than gold. However, towards the end of the factory's life, perhaps about 1825, some 'all-over' brightly coloured patterns in an Imari style were heightened or weighted by the addition of gold. The pair of vases (Plate 183) decorated in this style can hardly be to everyone's taste.

Silver lustre was also used as part of a few patterns. Since none of these were given a number they cannot be placed exactly in the pattern book although most of them appear on services featuring the boat-shaped teapot. It is likely that these pieces were made at the beginning of the nineteenth century (Plate 151).

By accident or design—probably the latter—when New Hall began they used coloured decoration from a palette whose range of bright, clean colours was excellent. The most likely reason for this is the wealth of experience and knowledge within the Warburton family. It is most likely that the factory had its own decorating shop from the earliest days at Shelton Hall, and this would be a bold innovation. Many Staffordshire potters used to send their wares to special decorating shops—like Ann Warburton's—and few before New Hall decorated on the premises in their own studio.

Throughout the hard-paste period the general style of enamel decoration was remarkably constant: only the quality and artistic merit changed. The patterns are recognised almost universally, and often erroneously, as being typical New Hall decoration. The simple borders were endless variations on the use of dots, lines, blobs and garlands whilst the main design was a collection of flowers. Few of the flowers have parallels in nature but this does not seem to affect the pleasing, naïve effect.

During the first decade very attractive polychrome patterns were used. These were mostly neat and of almost realistic flower sprays beneath a simple border (e.g. patterns 3 and 139) but a few *chinoiserie* designs are known (patterns 20 and 157).

The use of yellow and blue enamels at this time is worth noting because neither were easy colours to apply. In fact they soon disappeared from the palette and although they returned at a later date their colour was relatively poor and lifeless. The problem with blue enamel is its opacity or rather lack of it. A normal layer of enamel, if blue, does not obliterate the background and a thicker coat is needed. This extra thickness of enamel, however, readily chips off the glaze— a fault which occurs frequently with the blue border on pieces decorated with pattern 22.

The early polychrome patterns were very popular and many of them had a long life, e.g. 171, which is found on tea-sets made throughout the hard-paste period (Plate 50) as well as on bone-china services. As time went by the neatness and rhythm of the flower sprays diminished, and this again was probably a reflection of the public taste. By varying the colour or the border used for a given spray the number of different patterns was increased without much extra effort on the part of the designer. Thus we find two borders with the same spray (patterns 297 and 298) or the same border with different sprays (patterns 746 and 791). It is rather confusing, though, to find in one case two different monochrome and one polychrome version of a pattern given different numbers (367, 598, 599) whilst in another case only one number, 241, given to the polychrome and black monochrome versions of a single pattern. This must have caused difficulty and uncertainty at the factory if someone wanted extra pieces made to replace broken ones.

No doubt an attempt was made in the bone-china period to cater for different tastes and pockets. On the one hand we find perfunctory decoration (pattern 1084) and simple borders and on the other hand 'all over' designs, often on a powder blue background, featuring mazarine blue leaves outlined and decorated with gold and flowers and ornaments washed in with an orange colour (pattern 1373). Other styles of decoration featured bat-printed[1] sprays of flowers, or birds, washed over with coloured enamels (patterns 1511 and 1560). At its best the decoration was very attractive showing considerable artistic merit.

It is no surprise to find extensive use made of transfer- and bat-printing processes. How could a factory function successfully during the period 1781–1835 without taking advantage of the repetitive techniques which increased the speed and economy of reproducing a given design?

Underglaze blue transfer decoration was successfully applied to the hard-paste porcelain from the earliest days. It was a considerable achievement, since Bristol and Plymouth had been unsuccessful. The different firing schedule and manufacturing method developed by these Staffordshire potters created a suitably hard biscuit body to receive the transfer-print. However, the temperature needed for

[1] Bat-printing is a process of transfer-printing from engraved copper-plates in which a bat of gelatine takes the place of transfer tissue.

E. Teapot, covered sucrier and jug decorated with underglaze blue transfer-print. New Hall, hard-paste, c. 1782–7; ht. of teapot (without knob) 4½ in. National Museum of Wales. See pages 36, 42 and 57

maturing the glaze, as well as its composition, did not really suit the cobalt blue. At no time was the final colour comparable to the best product of the soft-paste factories.

The patterns were mostly of a willow-pattern type with Chinese pagodas, willow trees, a bridge with a man on it and various types of boats (Plates 191, 194, 195). Two of the commonest designs feature a pair of moth-like flying insects (Plate 196) and a row of 'drain-pipes' (Plate 192) which were probably meant to be a bamboo fence but which Dr. Watney has likened rather appropriately to trench mortars. Two of the rarer designs show children playing—a delightful scene (Plate 190)—and a flowering shrub with two flying doves above it. The latter design is coupled with a willow root and other pieces of the flowering shrub (Colour Plate E and Plate 189). One of the most interesting patterns incorporates a pagoda in a cleft rock (commonly called a gazebo). Rare pieces like leaf-shaped pickle-dishes (Plate 188) have been found bearing this decoration as well as a tea-service marked with the crowned Frankenthal lion mark (Plate 185).

Most of the borders, like those commonly found with willow patterns, are uninspired and also hard to distinguish. But one of overlapping pointed leaves which appears with the gazebo pattern (Plate 188) and another with trefoil shaped leaves hanging from the line border (Plate 189) are simple enough to be pleasing.

These blue transfer-prints were used almost throughout the hardpaste period since they are found applied to the majority of the different shapes, i.e. globular, 'silver-shape', boat-shape, oval-based straight-sided and waisted teapots. However, the real collector's interest is focused on the early pieces like the asparagus-servers, knife handles and leaf dishes. So far these pieces have been found with this type of decoration only.

Some underglaze transfers were used as outlines for overglaze decoration. Several different versions of the same pattern could then be marketed by adding different colour combinations (patterns 272, 274, 490, and 856—Plate 72).

On-glaze transfers were used to outline the Chinese courtyard scenes (patterns 425 and 621) and these were completed with enamel colours. When bat-printing was introduced, about 1800, a more detailed picture could be applied to the glaze and New Hall quickly began to use the new process (pattern 462—Plate 113). Then the pictures were coloured. Realistic country scenes, some actually named, were depicted and a tea-set would show several scenes (pattern 984). The name harlequin set has been given to these series. Various gilt borders were used to complete the decoration and these gave rise to different pattern numbers.

In 1810, Peter Warburton took out a patent for a method of printing these landscapes and country scenes in gold and platinum instead of the commonly used black. This decoration produces a handsome effect since the gold has usually mellowed beautifully. Mazarine blue borders with added gilt decoration were sometimes added but this makes the whole effect rather heavy (Plates 149 and 150).

On bone-china a popular series of printed patterns was based upon engravings designed by Adam Buck, the society portrait painter who exhibited frequently in the Royal Academy exhibitions from 1795 until his death in 1833. Different scenes of a mother and her child are depicted. The prints are found in black alone (pattern 1109) and with the print colour-washed over. The latter variant is sometimes within a gold circle and sometimes a vignette within a mazarine blue background (Colour Plate G). These four alternatives provided the customer with a wide price range from which to choose.

DECORATORS

The simplicity and straightforward nature of the majority of New Hall's decoration enabled a painter of ordinary skill to be employed as a decorator. Little artistic genius was needed beyond the ability to copy. It is not surprising then that the work of individual painters has not been recognised and signed pieces are at a premium. Anonymity is the fate of the painters who worked in the New Hall studio.

Fidelle Duvivier is the only painter whose work has been identified. He was probably responsible for creating the patterns used during the first decade. Born in Tournai in 1740 and learning his craft there, he spent most of his life decorating English porcelain. Besides working in London and at Worcester he is known to have been employed by William Duesbury for four years from 1769. Whilst working at Derby his son Peter Joseph was born: he was baptised there on 20th March 1771. In 1790 he wrote to William Duesbury:

'Hanley green, the 1 novebr 1790, Mr. Dousbery, Sir,—take the liberty Adressing you with a few lines, as mine engegement in the new Hal Porcelaine manufatory is Expierd, and the propriotors do not intend to do much more in the fine line of Painting, therefor think of Settling in new Castle under lime being engag'd to teech Drowing in the Boarding School at that place, one School I have at Stone, so as to have only three days to Spare in the week for Painting, which time Could wish to be employ'd by you preferable to eany other fabricque, because you like and understand good work, as am inform'd, my painting now, to watt I did for your father, is quit diferent but without flatering my Self, Hope to give you Satisfaction, in Case you Schould like to inploy me, Sir,—your anser will much oblige your Humble Servant, Duvivier.

P.S. the conveyance would be much in fevoir for to Send the ware to and from, as ther is a waggon Every week from darby to new Castle'

This letter quoted by Jewitt[1] is important since it proves that Duvivier worked at New Hall and was about to leave there in 1790. The comment 'do not intend to do much more in the fine line of Painting' is significant since by the date of this letter the simplified and streamlined range of potting shapes and with it, presumably, the style of decoration, had been introduced.

Most of the pieces whose decoration is attributed to this painter were made during the first period of production. The teapot (Plate 1) illustrated originally by Jewitt, was made, he said, for the partner Charles Bagnall and many of the cups in the Luton Museum collection belong to a tea-set with similar decoration. The tea-caddy and plate illustrated in colour (Colour Plate B) are good examples of Duvivier's palette and the delicate way in which the hazy distance scene is handled. On the back of the plate is a boldly painted 'No 5' in brown enamel which probably refers to the border pattern.

A coffee-cup with a thumb-rest handle signed 'F: · Duvivier fecit' (Plates 14 and 15) is evidence of this artist's style and the fact that he decorated New Hall porcelain. It has been suggested[2] that this brazen signature possibly indicates that it was decorated by the artist in his own atelier. If this is the case, the cup must have been stored for some years since it was surely made before 1790, the date when Duvivier wrote to Duesbury at Derby.

The large presentation jugs made about the turn of the century generally bear fine decoration (Colour Plate A) and were probably decorated outside the factory. Two of these jugs were almost certainly decorated by Duvivier (Plates 13 and 16). One specimen (Plate 13), with a bird and its nest on one side, is illustrated by Jewitt, who states that the initials S. D. were those of Samuel Daniel, a cousin of John Daniel, one of the partners. The Stoke-on-Trent Museum at Hanley has inherited this historic jug.

F. H. Rhead[3] names the three artists Henry Bone, Thomas Pardoe and Joshua Cristall as decorating New Hall porcelain but no further confirmatory evidence has been found. In fact apart from Duvivier no New Hall decorator has been positively identified.

[1] Ll. Jewitt, *op. cit.*, vol. 2, p. 97.   [2] R. J. Charleston, *op. cit.*, p. 158.
[3] *Connoisseur*, September 1916, p. 221.

MARKS

There was no factory mark during the hard-paste period. The occurrence of on-glaze Sèvres, Plymouth and Bristol marks is misleading and in most cases faked. Two tea-bowls in the Victoria and Albert Museum (pattern 153) have the Sèvres mark ⋏ in a bright blue colour which is atypical and the date in a gold whose soft easily-rubbed nature is different from the main gilt decoration. Also in the Victoria and Albert Museum are a coffee-cup and saucer both bearing a blue cross mark. The cup was made at New Hall (pattern 195) and the saucer was made by Factory X (decorated with their version of this pattern, see p. 101)! No doubt the mark was intended to seal the marriage of the two pieces and to ensure that they should live in a 'Bristol' cabinet.

Pattern numbers are the only regularly used marks which have been noted. These are found alone or accompanied by the letters 'N' or 'No'. The colour used is chosen quite arbitrarily and is not necessarily found in the pattern itself. This suggests that someone may have been deputed to put these numbers on the pieces, either before decoration to instruct the painter or after decoration to help the sorters assemble the orders. These numbers are found under the principal pieces of a service, i.e. teapot and stand, sugar-bowl, jug, basins and plates but never regularly under the tea-bowls, cups or saucers. In fact, the number of these latter pieces which bear a pattern number is so small that they constitute exceptions which prove the rule. It should be borne in mind that in the years of experimentation even these pattern numbers were rarely used. Their introduction was delayed until the late 1780's.

A few of the early blue-and-white pieces were marked with a crowned Frankenthal lion under the glaze, but this mark was not used regularly (Plate 185). Apparently the transfer-prints were not allotted a pattern number and consequently apart from the few lion marks these wares are unmarked.

Frequently painters' marks are found but they are unreliable guides to identification. However, it has been suggested[1] that three of these marks are typical. They are generally found on pieces made towards the end of the hard-paste period. The 'f' is also found on some of the early bone-china pieces.

During the bone-china period a factory identification mark was used. This was a transfer-print of two concentric rings surrounding the words '*New Hall*' in script. Sometimes it accompanied the pattern number on the important pieces of a service but more frequently it was applied to the saucers. Jewitt suggests that it was introduced after

[1] R. J. Charleston, *op. cit.*, p. 159.

The Frankenthal lion mark

The mark found on a few pieces of tea-services decorated with stipple prints in gold.

Bone-china marks

Workmen's marks

Newhall

G E F

Impressed mark and Patent Office Registration mark sometimes found on pieces made by Thomas Booth c. 1872–80.

NEWHALL

1820 and used sparingly but since it is found beneath many pieces decorated with early bone-china patterns (e.g. pattern 1109) the date of introduction was more likely to be 1815. Moreover, I am not convinced that 'sparingly' really describes their use.

A rare mark which I have seen only beneath a bone-china dessert-plate has '*Newhall*' in continuous script without the circles.

Finally I must mention an impressed mark of 'NEWHALL'. This is found beneath smear-glazed stoneware pieces and probably earthenware made by Thomas Booth and Sons who worked part of the New Hall premises between 1872 and 1880. A teapot with this mark is illustrated (Plate 184) and a jug in Canada has a registration mark giving 1867 as the date of registration of the pattern besides the name of the manufactory.

7

A RECONSTRUCTION OF PART OF
A NEW HALL PATTERN BOOK

No original book recording patterns used by New Hall has been found or recorded. But the association of particular numbers and patterns on New Hall porcelain points strongly to the factory's maintaining a pattern book. Furthermore, the obvious change and development in style of decoration and shape of wares with increasing pattern number indicate that patterns were added to the book in direct sequence.

Although we must not assume that the number of new patterns introduced each year was constant, the figure for an average yearly output is nevertheless useful. With cautious application such a figure has helped to build up and fill in the outline of the productive life of the factory.

Pattern number 1700 is the highest one which I have seen applied to a piece marked also with the concentric ring mark. However, some bone-china dessert-plates and tea-services of possible New Hall origin have been noted which bear pattern numbers up to 2270. These figures give an average annual pattern output of between thirty-one and forty-two.

It is a remarkable coincidence that the pattern book contained about one thousand different patterns when the factory changed from the manufacture of hard-paste to bone-china. This was not contrived, since patterns up to number 1048 have been seen on hard-paste, and the country scenes of pattern number 984 were applied more often to the bone-china than the hard-paste body.

Very few of the early wares were marked with a pattern number and the large 'silver-shape' and the oval-base, waisted teapots had been introduced before the numbers were applied regularly. This suggests that there was no pattern book during the first few years and that one was only made when the proprietors were confident of the success of their venture. It is possible also that they were speeded into this organisation by requests for repeat orders or for replacement pieces. Perhaps the introduction of a pattern book and the marking of pattern numbers were part of the rationalisation which was marked by the production of only standard services and the release of Duvivier?

Collectors must be very careful not to use the pattern on a piece of porcelain as an indicator of its date of manufacture. Since patterns were often used over a long period of time the only information to be gleaned from this source is a piece's earliest possible date. Its shape, and in some cases the nature of its paste and glaze, are the only true guides to its date.

The descriptions of the patterns given in the following pages are intended to be used in conjunction with the illustrations and only a few of them are self-sufficient. Frequently only the border and the main decoration are included since only these are common to most of the pieces of a service. The small, supplementary sprigs that complete a pattern usually vary in number and position on different pieces so that a generalisation here is impossible.

Interpretation of colour is individual and agreement is rarely possible when words replace the visual image. It is earnestly hoped that the colours recorded here can be recognised.

Pattern 3 (Plates 5 and 17)
   Border: Two pink bands between which are pink circles with blue dot centres. Main spray: A pink flower out of which grows a mauve flower and a stem of three mauve flowers; the leaves are in two different greens. Second spray: A blue pimpernel out of which grows a pink rose and a yellow bud.
   These sprays are known beneath different borders.

Pattern 20 (Colour Plate C, Plates 18, 19 and 20)
   Border: One straight and one arched iron-red line. Alternately, one magenta blob and four blue blobs are attached to the lower line. Main decoration: The figure with the iron-red parasol wears blue, magenta and yellow clothes, and the figure offering a magenta flower wears magenta, blue and yellow clothes.
   A sequel to this pattern shows only the person with the parasol who is also holding the flower.

Pattern 22 (Plates 17 and 21)
   Border: Plum-red criss-cross lines and dots between a blue line and a sequence of blue semi-circles. Main spray: A plum-red flower with a yellow centre behind which is a blue and yellow flower. There is also a yellow flower with iron-red stamens. The leaves are in two greens.

F. Teapot decorated in underglaze mazarine blue and gold (pattern 153)
New Hall, hard-paste, c. 1787–90; ht. 6½ in.
See pages 37 and 54

Pattern 52 (Plate 22)
All gold.

Pattern 64 (Plate 24)
All gold.

Pattern 67 (Plates 5 and 25)
Border: Magenta scale band between iron-red lines. Pendent from a pink rose with four green leaves are mauve swags in the centre of which are iron-red pimpernels.

Pattern 78 (Plates 26 and 27)
A variant of pattern 67 in which the scale border is broken with a mauve and magenta device.

Pattern 83 (Colour Plate D, Plates 12 and 28)
All gold except for the rose and foliage insets. The colour of the rose varies between pink and mauve and the foliage can be four simple leaves or delicate tracery and leaves.

Pattern 89 (Colour Plate D)
Border: Gold chain with a magenta line within each link and two magenta trefoils between each pair of links.

Pattern 98 (Plate 29)
Border: Undulating blue dot line intersecting a straight chain of two-tone green husks. A red dot between each husk. The rims are usually brown.

Pattern 121 (Plate 30)
Border: Iron-red bells have a spray of green leaves and pink and mauve florets hanging from them. These bells are linked by a mauve line with a magenta feather at each end. Magenta sprigs are scattered over the body of all pieces.

Pattern 122 (Plate 31)
Border: A chain of magenta hearts between two iron-red lines. Beneath the lower line are a straight and a looped line. Blue dots are within the loops. The other border is a green undulating line which crosses a chain of magenta hearts.

Pattern 133 (Plate 32)
Black border and pattern.

Pattern 136 (Plate 33)
All gold except for an orange dot in the centre of the flowers.

Pattern 139 (Plates 17 and 34)
Border: Magenta festoons linked by iron-red lines beneath a

straight iron-red line. Main spray: A realistic pink rose with a mauve flower behind. Green leaves.

Pattern 140 (Plate 35)
Border: Pale pink wash with a darker pink pattern of loops and dots painted over. On the outside is an iron-red line and on the inside a yellow-green line overpainted with a black zigzag line. Main spray: Pink rose with a mauve flower behind. Green leaves.

Pattern 141 (Plate 36)
The main scene is in orange-brown. The decoration around the frame is mainly blue and orange-brown. A pattern similar to this is known on pieces of porcelain made by Haynes at Swansea around 1796.

Pattern 142 (Plate 37)
Border: Curling brown feathers intersecting an undulating line of gold dots. The intersection is marked by large dots. All other rims and bands are plain gold.

Pattern 144 (Plate 38)
Border: A line of mauve dots below a single iron-red line and above a double iron-red line. Beneath this is an undulating line of green leaves and coloured flowers. Main spray: Back-to-back pink and mauve flowers. Green leaves.

Pattern 145 (Plate 39)
Decoration is all gold except for dark blue enamel at the bottom of each swag.
Caution. Some pieces in a service bearing apparently identical decoration have been noted which bore the number 245.

Pattern 152 (Plate 40)
Underglaze mazarine blue pattern completed with applied gold.

Pattern 153 (Colour Plate F)
Underglaze mazarine blue completed with overglaze gold decoration.

Pattern 154 (Plate 42)
The zigzag lines are in underglaze mazarine blue and all other decoration is overglaze gold.

Pattern 155 (Plate 43)
Underglaze mazarine blue band completed with overglaze gold decoration.

Pattern 157 (Plate 44)
Border: Iron-red. Main decoration: The two outside figures are

dressed in magenta, blue and yellow clothes but the central figure wears magenta trousers. The table is in iron-red. The foreground and leaves are in two shades of green.

Pattern 161 (Plate 45)
Border: Green leaves on mauve stems with blue and red buds between two gold lines. The sprigs on the body of the pieces are alternate gold and coloured.

Pattern 166 (Plate 46)
All of the festoon is gold. The single florets are in a soft green.

Pattern 167 (Plate 47)
Border: An apricot or peach coloured band between two gold lines set below the gold rim of the piece. The body of the piece is decorated with gold sprigs.
Patterns 206, 221, 222 and 258 are related.

Pattern 168 (Plate 48)
Very pale apricot festoons hang from the border used in pattern 167.

Pattern 170 (Plate 49)
Border: Dark blue scrolls are edged with gold. The rest of the decoration is gold.

Pattern 171 (Plates 50 and 51)
The basket pattern. Borders: Mauve dots between two iron-red lines. An undulating dotted and continuous brown line. Main spray: A brown basket filled with coloured flowers with green leaves.

Pattern 172 (Plate 51)
The mauve ribbon pattern. Border: Undulating mauve ribbon crossed by a magenta straight line. Beneath the mauve loops are magenta bristles and above the loops are alternately a sprig of a pink and mauve rose and a sprig of two iron-red buds. The body of the piece is scattered with coloured sprigs.

Pattern 173 (Plate 52)
Borders: Pink scale edged with two thin brown lines. Coloured sprays hang from this border; alternate ones contain a mauve rose bud. An undulating dotted and continuous brown line. The body of the piece is scattered with coloured sprigs.

Pattern 180
The body of the piece is scattered with gold stars. The only other decoration is a gold rim and a gold band around the footrim of appropriate pieces.

Pattern 181 (Plate 53)

Border: Pale green band with everything else gold.

Pattern 183 (Plate 54)

Border: Pink roses within gold ovals set in a band made up of green dots within mauve dotted ovals. All other decoration is gold.

Pattern 186 (Plate 55)

The pink ribbon pattern. Borders: Red undulating ribbon with coloured sprigs within the loops. Undulating green leaf line with occasional pink and mauve roses crossing two thin iron-red lines. Some junctions feature an iron-red star-like device. Most pieces have coloured sprigs scattered over the body.

Pattern 191 (Plate 56)

Border: Undulating green leaf line crossing two thin straight black lines. Magenta pimpernels appear at the intersections. Main spray: Coloured pimpernel-like flowers and green leaves.

Pattern 195 (Plate 57)

Border: A complex border which features iron-red string-like and magenta feather festoons. Main spray: A pink and a mauve rose, green leaves, two sprays of iron-red florets and a single pink rose.

Pattern 202 (Plates 59 and 60)

Border: Dark blue underglaze blobs with two magenta enamel petals behind. The rest of the decoration is gold.

Pattern 206 (Plate 61)

Border: A yellow band between two gold lines. The upper of these two lines is the rim of the piece (when a bowl or cup or saucer). The body of the piece is decorated with small gold sprigs.

Patterns 167, 221, 222 and 258 are related.

Pattern 208 (Plate 62)

Border: Undulating line of orange dots intersecting a continuous straight line of blue arrow-heads beneath a black line. Main spray: A green broad leaf separating two pink roses. Iron-red and mauve florets and green leaves complete the spray.

Pattern 213 (Plate 63)

The florets of the sprays are mainly pale blue with a few magenta lines added. The rest of the decoration is gold.

Pattern 221

Border: This is a modification of pattern 206. A yellow band with a gold and a black line above and a black line and a gold small leaf and berry edging. The whole is set below the gold rim of a piece.

Patterns 167, 206, 222 and 258 are related.

Pattern 222 (Plate 64)

Border: This is a modification of pattern 167. An apricot-peach band with a gold and a black line above and a black line and a gold small leaf and berry edging. The whole is set below the gold rim of a piece.

Patterns 167, 206, 221 and 258 are related.

Pattern 238 (Plate 65)

Border: The medallions are coloured with apricot-peach enamel and magenta trefoils are features. The rest of the decoration is gold.

Pattern 241 (Plate 66)

Border: Undulating red dotted line crossing another undulating line which features leaves and florets. Alternate crests show a pink rose and a pink pimpernel. Main spray: Back-to-back pink and mauve roses are the main feature. The upper green leaves are usually vigorously lance-like and the bottom pair of leaves are usually arranged almost horizontally and are iron-red in colour.

The same pattern number was used when the decoration was done in black only.

Pattern 245

See Pattern 145.

Pattern 248 (Plate 67)

Border: Underglaze mazarine blue band with the rest of the decoration gold.

Pattern 253 (Plate 68)

Borders: Mauve ornamental line within a thin iron-red line. Undulating plain iron-red and dotted mauve lines. Main spray: Back-to-back pink and mauve flowers with a flat-headed mauve flower and two green leaves growing out from them. Three iron-red leaves are featured beneath.

This decoration is also found in black and the same pattern number is used.

Pattern 258

Border: This is a pink version of pattern 206. A pink band is between two gold lines. The upper of these two lines is the rim of the piece (when a bowl or cup or saucer). The body of the piece is decorated with small gold sprigs.

Patterns 167, 206, 221 and 222 are related.

Pattern 259 (Plate 69)

Border: There are either blue or red dots within the spaces in the gold lattice. All other decoration is gold.

Pattern 266 (Plate 70)

Border: Most of this is gold. The more ornate festoons bear red berries and have a red quatrefoil at the bottom of the loop. The rest of the decoration is gold.

Pattern 267 (Plate 71)

Border: A thin iron-red line from which hangs a mauve undulating line. Main spray: Green leaves, a pink rose and a number of small coloured florets.

Pattern 272 (Plate 72)

Border: Narrow, smudged underglaze blue transfer-print. The over-all pattern is an underglaze blue transfer-print with some of the leaves and flowers coloured with orange, magenta and green enamels on top of the glaze.

Patterns 274, 490 and 856 are related.

Pattern 273 (Plate 73)

Border: Magenta scale between a thick magenta and a thin iron-red line. Below this latter is a mauve looped line from which hang small magenta buds and three small green leaves. Main spray: The centre is a pink rose behind which is half of a deep mauve flower. There are green leaves and a small pink rose as well as some iron-red florets.

Pattern 274 (Plate 72)

This pattern is the same as pattern 272 to which has been added a considerable amount of gold. This is mostly to outline the border and the many leaves in the pattern.

Patterns 272, 490 and 856 are related.

Pattern 280 (Plate 74)

Border: An undulating black line to which are attached black and gold trefoils and gold and magenta dots.

Pattern 288 (Plate 75)

Border: Gold design and lines. Magenta or orange dots are attached to the undulating gold line. The sprigs, which are usually scattered on the body of pieces, are magenta (or orange) and gold. The centres of saucers usually feature an attractive magenta (or orange) foxglove-like flower with gold leaves.

Pattern 289

Border: Orange-brown band within two gold lines. The rest of the decoration is gold.

Patterns 306 and 307 are related.

Pattern 290 (Plate 76)

Border: All gold except for the florets, which are mauve.

Pattern 291 (Plate 77)

Border: All gold except for large orange dots and groups of three berries, each of which has some added black decoration.

Pattern 294

Border and spray painted in black enamel.
Pattern 295 is related.

Pattern 295 (Plates 78 and 237)

Border and spray identical in design to that used for pattern 294. Colour is orange (sometimes iron-red) enamel.

Pattern 297 (Plate 79)

Border: An interrupted orange band from which is scratched a zig-zag line between two thin black lines. The interruptions are mauve stems leading to a pink floret and three pairs of green leaves. Main spray: A mauve multi-petalled flower with an iron-red centre, a pink flower and a spray of four iron-red florets with green leaves in two shades.
Pattern 298 is related.

Pattern 298 (Plate 80)

The same spray as pattern 297. Border: A thin iron-red line and a thin mauve line to which is attached by pink flower buds an un-dulating mauve line. There are blue dots beneath the pink flower buds.
Pattern 297 is related.

Pattern 306 (Plate 81)

Border: Mazarine blue band within two gold lines. The rest of the decoration is gold.
Patterns 289 and 307 are related.

Pattern 307

Border: Pink band within two gold lines. The rest of the decoration is gold. This is a colour variant of pattern 306.
Patterns 289 and 306 are related.

Pattern 308 (Plate 82)

All decoration in black enamel.
Pattern 328 is the same design carried out in coloured enamels.

Pattern 311 (Plate 83)

Border: Three thin iron-red lines. Between the outer two is a row of pink arrow-heads and groups of three dots. Between the inner two is pink scale interrupted by vignettes painted in black. The larger ones contain two iron-red rose buds on the black foliage. The remainder of the piece is covered with scattered sprigs. The central sprig has only one pink rose. The leaves are painted in two shades of green.

Pattern 312 (Plate 84)

Border: Iron-red line beneath which is a feathery mauve line joining deep pink flowers with four pairs of leaves. Main spray: A deep pink rose and three puce-coloured pansy-like flowers amidst leaves of two shades of green. A pink flower bursting from its green bud climbs upwards from the group.

Pattern 317 (Plate 85)

Border: Between gold lines, the upper of which is on the rim of the piece are light purple leaves and alternate gold and iron-red flowers.

Pattern 319 (Plate 86)

Border: The central panel contains two bunches of purple grapes and the florets in the adjacent panels are blue. All the rest of the decoration is gold.

Pattern 336 (Plate 87)

All the decoration is in blue enamel on the glaze.

Pattern 338 (Plate 88)

Border: Mauve undulating line interrupted by sprays containing a pink rose. Main spray: A wheel painted with black, pink, orange, pink, etc. sections within a wreath of pink roses, orange pimpernels and leaves painted in two shades of green.

Pattern 339 (Plate 89)

Border: The florets in the foliage are mainly blue with magenta lines added. All the rest is gold except for some of the dots on the lower undulating line which are magenta.

Pattern 343 (Plate 90)

Mazarine blue underglaze band with all other decoration done in gold.

Pattern 353 (Plate 91)

Border: Inside on the mug, but usually outside on a tea-bowl, there is a chain of green and mauve. Outside the mug but inside tea-bowls is mauve-magenta decoration beneath a thin black line. Main spray: Pink and mauve flowers with two shades of green-coloured leaves.

G. Teapot decorated with a bat-print of a mother and child scene
after engravings by Adam Buck (pattern 1277)
New Hall, bone-china, c. 1815–25; ht. 6 in. See page 58

Pattern 354 (Plate 92)

Border: Red scale patches outlined with thin black lines and beneath a thin black line. A continuous line of magenta arrowheads. Main spray: Pink and mauve back-to-back roses are the main feature.

A 'silver-shape' teapot in the Victoria and Albert Museum is decorated with this pattern and the words 'Sophia Sayer 1803'.

Pattern 363 (Plate 93)

Border: The florets and buds are mauve. Some have yellow centres. The rest of the decoration is gold.

Pattern 366 (Plate 94)

Border: Mostly iron-red. The sprigs on the border contain pink, mauve and iron-red florets and green leaves. Main spray: Rather insignificant florets tied with iron-red strings.

Pattern 367 (Plate 95)

Decoration all in black enamel.
Patterns 598 and 599 are related.

Pattern 373 (Plate 96)

The decoration rambles round the bowl in *famille rose* style. The flowers are coloured with orange, pink and blue enamels, the leaves are green.

Pattern 376 (Plate 97)

The sprays in the border and the main spray of the pattern feature a pink rose and two yellow centred flowers amongst green leaves and florets coloured blue and blue with yellow centres. Mauve sprigs are scattered over the rest of the pieces.

Pattern 377 (Plate 98)

Main spray: The star-shaped flower is magenta with blue and then yellow within. The buds are light brown with black dotted outline and the leaves are green with black marks painted on them.

Pattern 398 (Plate 99)

Border: The framework is gold and the background of some sections is coral-pink. The flowers in the large frame are a bright magenta-red.

A similar pattern is often referred to as the 'Church Gresley' pattern.

Pattern 415 (Plate 202)

Border: Blue rim line. Black festoons; one set of these has yellow and green enamel decoration added.

Pattern 420 (Plate 100)

Decoration is in black enamel.

Pattern 421 (Plate 101)

Border: Iron-red. Foreground and background are black and iron-red. Boy has a magenta top and green trousers. Middle figure is all blue. Right figure has a green gown on top of a red skirt.

Pattern 431 depicts the same group of people wearing different coloured clothes.

Pattern 422 (Plate 102)

All the pattern is painted with blue and pink enamels. Most of the flowers are blue and the leaves and stems pink. The rim band is blue or gold.

Pattern 425 (Plate 103)

The window pattern.

Pattern 431

The middle figure has a magenta top and a yellow skirt and the right-hand figure has a green gown on top of a blue underskirt. The pattern and all other colours are the same as for pattern 421.

Pattern 434 (Plate 104)

Border: Brown rim band. Iron-red tendrils and stems have blue flowers and light green leaves on them.

Pattern 437 (Plate 105)

The undulating line is mauve. All other decoration is gold.

Pattern 445 (Plate 106)

Border: The fuchsia-like flowers are underglaze blue with pink enamel lines around the edges. The rest of the decoration is gold.

Pattern 446 (Plate 107)

The tree and its base leaves are in underglaze blue and outlined with gold. The berries are orange. Other leaves are formed with grey stems and red dots and outlined with gold dots.

Pattern 449 (Plate 108)

Border: Chains of pimpernels and leaves between large orange-brown blobs. Main spray: Pink and mauve back-to-back flowers are in the centre of the spray, which is within a magenta line frame.

Pattern 450 (Plate 109)

Border: Undulating purple line crossing with an undulating chain of leaves and small flowers. Main spray: Back-to-back pink and mauve flowers are at the centre.

Pattern 455 (Plate 110)
Decoration is all in orange.

Pattern 459 (Plate 111)
Border: A broad orange-pink band with all other decoration in gold.

Pattern 461 (Plate 112)
All the decoration is in black.

Pattern 462 (Plate 113)
The decoration includes a wide variety of black stipple prints. The nature of the gold border affects the pattern number. Pattern 462 has a thin gold line beneath the thick gold rim band.

Patterns 466 and 511 have different gold borders and pattern 709 has no gold but only black lines added to the same series of stipple prints.

Pattern 466 (Plate 114)
A border variant of pattern 462.

Pattern 467 (Plate 115)
Borders: Top border is iron-red band overdrawn with black lines. Lower border is iron-red lines and ribbon with coloured florets and leaves in alternate loops. Main spray: The colours used are darker than usually painted being mostly magenta and purple. Two shades of green are used for the leaves.

Pattern 471 (Plate 116)
Border: The blossoms are painted pale blue with red tendrils. The rest of the pattern is gold.

Pattern 472 (Plate 117)
Border: The left-hand end of each panel is washed in with mauve enamel and the rest of the decoration is black enamel. There is a gold rim band.

Pattern 480 (Plate 118)
Decoration is all gold.

Pattern 490 (Plate 72)
This pattern utilises the same pale blue underglaze transfer outline design as patterns 272 and 274. Some of the leaves are coloured with a dark underglaze blue. Less magenta enamel colour is used. The border is an underglaze mazarine blue band with a continuous leaf and berry motif in gold between two gold lines.

Patterns 272, 274 and 856 are related.

Pattern 499 (Plate 119)
Border: A deep underglaze mazarine blue band with overglaze gold decoration.

Pattern 511 (Plate 120)
Black stipple print designs with a characteristic gold border.
Patterns 462, 466 and 709 use the same stipple prints with different borders.

Pattern 524 (Plate 121)
Underglaze mazarine blue leaves and acorns. The rest of the decoration is gold.

Pattern 530 (Plate 122)
A courtyard scene decorated in coloured enamels.

Pattern 533 (Plate 123)
Underglaze mazarine blue band. Green and yellow bunches of grapes. The rest of the decoration is gold.

Pattern 540 (Plate 124)
Underglaze mazarine blue background and outline to the leaves and flowers in the pattern. Decoration completed with gold.

Pattern 541 (Plate 125)
Border: Magenta scale areas from a black line band. Main spray: Tall iron-red vase with a spray of flowers and leaves. Two magenta coloured flowers, one above the other, are the main feature.

Pattern 550 (Plate 126)
The animal and trees are in underglaze dark blue and outlined and decorated with gold lines and dots. The animal has a red mouth and there are some red dots in the background.

Pattern 558
Orange ground colour variant of pattern 695.

Pattern 562 (Plate 127)
The leaves, acorns and flower in underglaze dark blue. The rest of the decoration in gold.

Pattern 575 (Plate 128)
Background of the pattern in underglaze dark blue. The rest of the decoration in gold.

Pattern 581 (Plate 129)
Background of the pattern in dark blue under the glaze. The rest of the pattern in gold.

Pattern 583 (Plate 130)
Background framework in underglaze dark blue. The rest of the decoration in gold.

Pattern 593 (Plate 131)
Border: Pale hatching with magenta devices in the insets. Main spray: The main flower and the two florets to its left are pink. Attached to these flowers are blue florets or leaves (five). Climbing out of the spray at the top is a small pansy in mauve and yellow. The leaves are in two shades of green.

Pattern 594 (Plate 132)
Border: Painted in iron-red. Main spray: The very rambling spray features flowers in orange and yellow. The leaves are in two shades of green.

Pattern 596 (Plate 133)
Border: Iron-red line with a magenta line beneath. From this latter hang swags of green and magenta dots and arrow-heads. Main spray: Magenta flower with iron-red centre and a broad green leaf. Other leaves in two shades of green.

Pattern 598
Decoration all in orange enamel on the glaze.
    Patterns 367 and 599 are related.

Pattern 599
Borders: Orange undulating dotted line with alternate blue and magenta florets hanging in alternate loops. The other chain is orange. Main spray: Large magenta rose and leaves in two shades of green.
    Patterns 367 and 598 have the same border and spray but they are painted in monochrome.

Pattern 603 (Plate 134)
Border: Pairs of broad brown leaves are linked by green leaf and floret loops and pendents. Small pink roses are on the ends of the pendents. Main spray: The two flowers are brown and magenta. The leaves are in two shades of green.

Pattern 621 (Plate 135)
An oriental scene sometimes referred to as 'dinner is served'.
    Pattern 673 is related.

Pattern 631 (Plate 123)
The leaves and bunches of grapes are in underglaze dark blue. The outlines and the rest of the decoration are in gold.

Pattern 660
Variant of pattern 748 in which the funnel-like devices are blue.

Pattern 662 (Plate 136)
Border: An interrupted orange band from which is scratched a zigzag line and on which are painted blue dots. Blue dots and angled lines are attached to the orange scalloped line. Main spray: This features a magenta rose and a flower with five purple petals and a yellow centre.

Pattern 673
A variant of pattern 621 in which the magenta scale and orange coloured framework to the picture have been replaced mainly by gold. The border is a narrow chain of iron-red dotted circles between two thin black lines.

Pattern 686 (Plate 137)
Border: Magenta scale band between two iron-red lines. Main spray: Puce and magenta back-to-back flowers.

Pattern 692 (Plate 138)
Underglaze mazarine blue band on top of which is the gold pattern.

Pattern 695 (Plate 138)
Mazarine blue underglaze background. The rest of the decoration is gold.
Pattern 558 is the same design on an orange ground.

Pattern 709
Black stipple prints. All line decoration is in black.
Patterns 462, 466 and 511 use the same stipple prints but are completed with different gold decoration.

Pattern 737 (Plate 123)
Leaves in underglaze dark blue. The bunches of grapes are orange. The rest of the decoration is gold.

Pattern 746 (Plate 139)
Border: Magenta arrow-heads and dots in sequence between two thin black lines. Magenta scale decoration fills in between simple enamel flower sprays. Main spray: Orange-brown basket and a blue ribbon. Main flower is magenta.
Pattern 791 uses the same border but has a different spray.

Pattern 748 (Plate 140)
Border: Orange and brown funnel-like devices are linked with leaf

and floret chains. Main spray: Single magenta rose and green leaves in two shades.

Pattern 660 is related.

Pattern 764
Mauve enamel decoration.

Pattern 779 (Plate 141)
Mazarine blue underglaze background. Green and yellow bunches of grapes. The rest of the decoration in gold.

Pattern 791
The same border decoration as pattern 746. Main spray: Single pink rose among green leaves in two shades. This spray was used for pattern 748.

Pattern 827 (Plate 142)
Underglaze mazarine blue framework outlined with gold. The orange trefoils have black lines on them and the rest of the sprays are gold.

Pattern 839 (Plate 143)
Border: Thin iron-red line. Undulating green leafed line with attached magenta florets alternating with pairs of blue dotted florets. There is no main spray.

Pattern 846 (Plate 150)
Border: Mazarine blue underglaze completed with gold. The decoration consists of some of the stipple prints used for patterns 462, 466, 511 and 709 applied in gold using Warburton's patented process.

Pattern 888 uses the same gold stipple prints within a different mazarine blue and gold border.

Pattern 856 (Plate 72)
The underglaze pale blue transfer-print first applied on pattern 272 is used for this pattern. Underglaze mazarine blue is used as an overall background and much of the pattern is left unpainted. The leaves which are painted are treated with orange and green. The whole of the decoration is completed with gold.

Patterns 272, 274 and 490 use the same pattern outline.

Pattern 888
Gold stipple print decoration applied by the Warburton patented process. A different underglaze mazarine blue and gold border from pattern 846 is used.

Pattern 901 (Plate 144)

The florets have five underglaze blue, five overglaze orange and five gold petals. The rest of the decoration is gold.

Pattern 914 (Plate 145)

Large pink realistic roses and green leaves. The rest of the decoration is gold.

Pattern 940 (Plate 146)

Blue rim line. The rambling spray features a large blue flower which has eight petals with an iron-red inner line. The three florets to the right of this flower have yellow centres. The flower on the left features five yellow dots with black outlines. These are attached to another blue and iron-red petalled head.

Pattern 947 (Plate 147)

Border: Pink band overpainted with pink lines and dots and interrupted by yellow moths outlined in black. This band is between iron-red lines. Main spray: Large yellow flower surrounded by green and iron-red leaves and tendrils.

Pattern 953 (Plate 148)

Border: Iron-red rim and line. Magenta roses and knots. Mauve dotted loops and feathers. Main spray: Single magenta rose and green leaves in two shades.

Pattern 984 (Plates 153 and 154)

The decoration is a large series of stipple prints which are coloured over with enamels. The range of subjects seems to be limitless. Ordinary country scenes are common and these include milkmaids and cows under trees. More interesting prints are of named places and may have been made as special orders.

This pattern is found on both the hard-paste and the bone-china bodies.

Patterns 1053 and 1063 are related.

Pattern 1040 (Plate 155)

Coloured enamels.

Pattern 1043 (Plate 156)

The florets are blue and orange. The rest of the decoration is gold.

Pattern 1045 (Plate 157)

Yellow shells. The orange-red trefoils have black centre marks.

A similar pattern was used by many other factories.

Pattern 1046 (Plate 158)

The decoration is mainly gold with additions in iron-red enamel.

H. Bone-china wares painted in enamels (pattern 1597). New Hall, bone-china, c. 1820–30; diam. of open dish 5 in. City Museum and Art Gallery, Stoke-on-Trent. See pages 48 and 55

Pattern 1053

The same stipple prints which were used for pattern 984 washed over with coloured enamels. The scenes are enclosed within two circles—the outer one gold and the inner one black.

Pattern 1054 (Plate 159)

Most of the decoration is carried out in a pale blue and a dark blue. The whole is completed with gold.

Pattern 1214 is related.

Pattern 1058 (Plate 160)

Main flower in the spray is a pink-red rose within blue-green and yellow-green leaves.

Pattern 1063

Black transfer-prints. Some are of classical subjects and others of country scenes as used in pattern 984. All rims and lines are black.

Pattern 1064 (Plate 161)

The flowers from left to right are in pink, yellow and brown enamels. The tendrils are in blue.

Pattern 1084 (Plates 162 and 163)

Decoration in orange and blue enamels.

This decoration was used by some other factories.

Pattern 1109

Black transfer-prints of scenes of a mother and her child taken from original works of Adam Buck. Rim and line decoration is black.

Patterns 1147, 1178, 1236, 1277 and 1525 are related.

Pattern 1147

Black transfer-prints of mother and child scenes which are similar to those used on pattern 1109 but the engraving is heavier. There is a very heavy gold border decoration added.

The workman's mark 'f' is sometimes found on these pieces.

Patterns 1109, 1178, 1236, 1277 and 1525 are related.

Pattern 1161 (Plate 164)

The leaves are in underglaze dark blue and the whole decoration is completed with gold. The five-petalled flowers have orange centres and are filled in with dots.

Pattern 1172 (Plate 165)

Oriental design in coloured enamels.

Pattern 1178

The same heavily engraved version of the mother and child scenes

G

as was used for pattern 1147. The gold borders on this pattern are not so heavy or ornate as found on pattern 1147.

Patterns 1109, 1147, 1236, 1277 and 1525 are related.

Pattern 1180 (Plate 166)
The bright pink border between blue lines is the most characteristic feature of this pattern.

Pattern 1214
The overall picture is in similar pale blue and dark blue colours as were used for pattern 1054. The elephant of pattern 1054 is here replaced by a pouncing lion.

Pattern 1236
The mother and child engravings used for pattern 1109 are coloured in with overglaze enamels. A gold line and border are added.

Patterns 1109, 1147, 1178, 1277 and 1525 are related.

Pattern 1277 (Colour Plate G)
The mother and child engravings are coloured with overglaze enamels in the same way as is found on pattern 1236. The scenes are set in vignettes surrounded by an underglaze mazarine blue background. The whole decoration is completed with gold.

Patterns 1109, 1147, 1178, 1236 and 1525 are related.

Pattern 1373 (Plate 167)
The decoration is surrounded by a mazarine blue and gold border and set against a pale blue background. The tree stem and leaves are in underglaze mazarine blue. The upper right flower is orange-brown and the one on the lower right has yellow petals surrounding a magenta centre. The whole decoration is completed with gold.

Pattern 1397
Illustrated in Colour Plate H.

Pattern 1442 (Plate 168)
The rims of all pieces are painted with yellow-orange enamel. The main spray features a mauve flower with a yellow centre and a smaller yellow flower.

Pattern 1478 (Plates 169 and 170)
Dessert-services with this relief moulded decoration—white on a pale blue background are usually given this pattern number. The central decoration on plates and dishes varies. Baskets of fruit, baskets of flowers and sprays of flowers are recorded.

Patterns 1480 and 1506 are related.

Pattern 1480 (Plate 171)

The background to the moulding and decoration is pink.
Patterns 1478 and 1506 are related.

Pattern 1485 (Plate 172)

The large flower in this decoration is pink.

Pattern 1506

This pattern number is given to dessert-services which have the
white relief moulding found on patterns 1478 and 1480 but in this
case the background is a dark green. The central decoration is
usually flowers.

Pattern 1511 (Plate 173)

Yellow-orange rim line. Branch in brown with a green and then
a brown leaf on either side of a magenta flower. The bird has a
mauve tail.

Pattern 1525 (Plate 174)

The mother and child engravings used for pattern 1109 are coloured
in with overglaze enamels in the same way as they are for pattern
1236. A single gold line near the rim is the only other applied
decoration.
Patterns 1109, 1147, 1178, 1236 and 1277 are related.

Pattern 1542 (Plate 175)

Border: Underglaze dark blue flowers with overglaze gold leaves
and tendrils. Pattern: Underglaze dark blue stems and leaves outlined with gold. Orange-brown flowers with green leaves. Occasional magenta flowers with yellow centres.

Pattern 1547 (Plate 176)

Blue and red flowers amongst green leaves.

Pattern 1560 (Plate 177)

Magenta rim line. Complex overglaze printed flower spray coloured
with enamels.

Pattern 1623 (Plate 178)

Decoration in purple enamel.

Pattern 1680 (Plate 179)

Border: Underglaze dark blue blobs connected by overglaze gold
leaves and tendrils. Pattern: Leaves in underglaze dark blue
outlined with gold and connected by gold tendrils. The main
flower has three large magenta-pink petals, a yellow centre and
purple berry-like dots.

Pattern 1681 (Plate 180)

Border: Underglaze blue band with applied leaf and berry motif in gold. Pattern: The ground and tree are in underglaze dark blue outlined with gold. The branches have orange-brown florets completed with gold. Both birds have magenta and yellow breasts, dark blue wings and orange tail feathers.

Part II

THE IMITATORS

PART II—THE IMITATORS

In the ceramic world it is difficult to condemn any particular factory as being an imitator of another, for who was original? Possibly the Chinese, since much English porcelain has a Chinese analogue. On the other hand most teapot and cream-jug shapes were made also by contemporary silversmiths.

What I intend to do in this section of the book is to draw attention to the factories which used similar shapes and decorations to those produced at New Hall. Some like Chamberlain's at Worcester, Caughley and Coalport, Minton, Spode and Mason are already quite well known and although New Hall almost certainly used the teapot shapes first, these factories cannot be called true imitators; they were only using and modifying contemporary shapes and patterns. The other factories which I have been able to classify but not identify can be said with truth to be imitators. Two of them used the New Hall hard-paste, the New Hall 'silver-shape' teapot and similar sprig patterns and borders. Furthermore they did not disclose their identity.

8

CHAMBERLAIN

Robert Chamberlain, who broke away from the original Worcester factory in about 1786, started on his own by decorating porcelain which he bought in the white from Caughley and other factories. Although some writers have suggested that Chamberlain bought porcelain from New Hall I have been unable to find any evidence to substantiate this claim. In about 1791 he began to make his own porcelain, using contemporary shapes. Most of his decoration was gilt (often over mazarine blue) but he also used coloured enamels. One of the coloured patterns closely resembles New Hall's number 241.

There were two styles of ware similar to those made at New Hall. One was the oval, waisted teapot with spiral fluting, whose handle had raised moulding on the outside and a small internal cusp (Plate 197). On this teapot the spout had straight flutes running the whole length and the knob had curved ridges which were usually picked out in gold. The ridges between the flutes on the body are often found to have a shallow groove running along them.

The sucrier (Plate 198) had a similar knob to that applied to the teapot lid and a trough ran beneath the lid's flat top. The mock handles, unlike those on a New Hall sucrier, were completely attached to the body, having been included in the original body mould.

The cream-jug (Plate 197), with a moulded handle similar to that on the teapot, was unlike any New Hall cream-jug.

New Hall's spiral fluting can usually be distinguished from that of other factories by its comparatively leisurely appearance. That featured on Chamberlain's wares approaches this gentleness but can be distinguished by the position of the top end of a given curve being displaced well to the right of its beginning near the footrim.

The other similar shape was the modification of the boat-shaped teapot which had an evenly curved collar around the top but no prow (Plate 199). The top of the handle with its forward pointing thumb-rest was separated from the body by a small strut. As a general rule this shape is found more frequently as a non-New Hall piece than a genuine one.

The handles on the sugar-pot (Plate 200), and on the cream-jug (Plate 200), are sufficiently distinctive for identification purposes.

Little has been written about the paste used by Chamberlain except the generalisation that it is of a cold, grey, hard texture and that the glaze on many pieces is disfigured by black spots. The black spots, which are caused by an accumulation of dirt in burst gas bubbles, are easily explained.

What about the paste?

The only analysis done has been published by Eccles and Rackham.[1] A plate marked 'Chamberlain's Worcester N 95' was taken and the figures (cf. p. 30) showed a silica/alumina ratio of 75.36/18.87. This was close enough to the result they obtained from a New Hall specimen to make them suggest that this piece was made by New Hall but decorated at Chamberlain's factory. Perhaps this is the origin of the story that Chamberlain decorated wares bought 'in the white' from New Hall.

Results from X-ray diffraction pattern investigations which I have made suggest that much Chamberlain porcelain is of a hard-paste nature (i.e. made from china-clay and china-stone) although some other ingredient, like a glass frit, may also have been added. It is my opinion that Chamberlain did not buy any wares from New Hall but made his own hard-paste type of body.

Chamberlain began to fire his own wares after 1791 and if he used this hard-paste body at that time, then he did it either illegally or under licence. I am inclined to think that he did neither but made his hard-paste type of body only after 1796, which would perhaps give some significance to the recorded teapot which is marked on the base with the date 1796.[2]

[1] Herbert Eccles and Bernard Rackham, *Analysed Specimens of English Porcelain*, No. 20.

[2] G. A. Godden, *An Illustrated Encyclopaedia of British Pottery and Porcelain*, 1966, Plate 104, p. 58.

9

LATE CAUGHLEY AND
EARLY COALPORT

Thomas Turner's Caughley factory, which was situated in pleasant rural surroundings on a hilltop above the River Severn near Broseley, is best known for underglaze blue-and-white decoration applied to a soapstone body. Turner sold this factory to John Rose of Coalport in 1799.

John Rose is said to have been apprenticed to Turner and after leaving him to have started making porcelain on his own account by the river at nearby Coalport. When he bought the Caughley factory in 1799 Rose did not rationalize production immediately but continued to use the works at the top of the hill until about 1814, when it was demolished. From that date all production was localised at Coalport.

In recent years the original Caughley site has been excavated and the wasters found used to prove the origin of many shapes of tea-wares which previously had been either wrongly attributed or merely unidentified. It has been the writer's good fortune to be involved in this work.[1]

The most important fundamental discovery made was that a hard-paste porcelain body as well as the original soapstone body was made at the Caughley factory. Furthermore, since the analysed sherds were unglazed biscuit, there was proof that hard-paste porcelain could be made by the high temperature biscuit and lower temperature glaze process. The evidence that this manufacturing process was possible is strong support for the contention that New Hall porcelain was made in this way.

Unfortunately we cannot be certain yet whether the production of the hard-paste body at Caughley was introduced by Turner or Rose. Although Turner tried unsuccessfully before 1790 to buy china-stone in Cornwall,[2] no contracts have yet come to light to show when, or

---

[1] *E.C.C. Trans.*, Vol. 6, Part 3, 1967, pp. 268–83.
[2] R. M. Barton, *A History of the Cornish China Clay Industry*, 1966, p. 35.

from where, this material was first bought. If the New Hall patent was enforced, then no hard-paste porcelain could have been made before 1796, which leaves a mere three years in which Turner could have made it. Therefore, little of the hard-paste wares can strictly be called Caughley.

An obvious solution is to call the first hard-paste wares Caughley-Coalport until it can definitely be established whether Turner or Rose owned the factory when they were made. The later hard-paste wares which were made when the factory was under John Rose's management should be called Coalport.

The collector's first problem occurs because many of the coloured patterns used on this hard-paste porcelain were either direct copies of existing New Hall patterns or were painted in a similar style. Confusion is increased by the use of some similar shapes. Perhaps the word imitator is justified here.

Like Chamberlain's at Worcester, the first teapot shape was oval-based, waisted and with spiral fluting (Plate 206). If Turner made any hard-paste porcelain then this shape must have been his and can be called Caughley. Certain features of this teapot can be proved as Caughley by matching sherds (Plate 205). The footrim is shallow and the fluting on the spout only goes half-way. The handle has an internal cusp but no moulding on the outside as had the Chamberlain model. On the lid there is an obvious groove between the fluted part and the plateau for the knob which, incidentally, has straight ridges on it. The most important features of the matching sucrier are the mock ring-handles which are part of the body. It should be recalled that New Hall specimens have applied rings which usually leave some space between the rings and the body of the sucrier.

The cream-jug which went with this tea-service is immediately distinguished from the New Hall jug by the shape of the handle (Plate 207). Further inspection shows that the proportions are different and that the neck is pressed in behind the spout. This style of jug was used also by Rose at Coalport with a later teapot shape (Plate 208).

There were plain, reeded and faceted variants of this service. However, although the teapots and sucriers have similar handles, spout and lid characteristics, the bulbous body is not waisted, a feature which went so well with spiral fluting.

Two other shapes of teapot are worth mentioning. One of these is common to many factories of the time, including New Hall, but the other originated from the Caughley factory under John Rose's Coalport management.

An oval-based teapot with straight vertical sides was made by Coalport, Miles Mason, Minton and Spode as well as New Hall.

Usually differences in the shape of the handle, spout, lid and knob are sufficient to identify the maker. The paste and the glaze also differ, but the experience of handling many pieces is essential. The style and nature of the decoration is the last feature to be considered, since a number of identical patterns were used by several factories. On the other hand, in some cases, although the patterns are different, similar coloured festoon borders and back-to-back roses were incorporated.

Coalport designed and developed a teapot whose spout was an integral part of the body (Plate 209). In fact its appearance suggests that one end of the body was drawn out to form this spout. The handle had a characteristic shape which at a later stage was modified to include a small internal strut near the bottom. Wasters found on the old Caughley site have proved the origin of these shapes, which are made from the hard-paste body. A service whose decoration includes the date 1807 helps to place it in the contemporary scene. The handles on the cream-jugs (Plate 211) were similar to those on the teapots but dolphin (Plate 210) or lion heads with a ring through the mouth were used on the covered sugar-pots.

Enamel decoration on these hard-paste Coalport pieces started in the New Hall style and often used the same patterns, e.g. New Hall numbers 195, 241, 267, 311 and 312. On the other hand, two of the patterns illustrated appear to have been used only by Coalport and almost certainly never by New Hall. Occasionally a pattern number is found beneath one or two pieces of a service and this is often in a bright green enamel. The number 74 was given to their copy of New Hall's number 195, and 77 to New Hall's number 312. Some of the later services were covered with flamboyant gilt decoration which was a reflection of the current taste and fashion. For instance, a copy of New Hall's pattern number 446 is known. Although some of these services must have been decorated at the factory, many were painted in London studios. Evidence of one of these (Baxter's) is found in a water-colour painting in the Victoria and Albert Museum.

10

MINTON

Thomas Minton founded the family business in Stoke-on-Trent in 1793. Since he was born in Shrewsbury it is not unexpected that we should discover he learnt about the manufacture of porcelain at Caughley; he was an apprentice engraver to Thomas Turner.

He is said to have worked in London, after leaving Turner, and then in Stoke with Josiah Spode before starting the Minton factory, which is still making fine porcelain. It is ironical to find that two members of the Hollins family were linked with the Mintons (page 12); and yet one of the probable causes of the decline of New Hall was a lack of family continuity.

A year or two after 1796 Minton's began to make porcelain. At first the body was whiter and more compact than the New Hall hard-paste and later, like that of all other factories, it contained bone ash.

It is not surprising that contemporary shapes and styles of decoration were being used for the early ware. The *chinoiserie* of pattern number 105 cannot really be confused with New Hall's number 425 (or the one used by Mason (Plate 201)) but the Minton looped pattern (number 18) is exactly the same as New Hall's number 415. The present-day Minton factory owns some of the early pattern books so that it is often possible to confirm Minton as the maker of a piece if it is marked with a pattern number. Even in the early years these numbers were added to most of the pieces in a tea-service, including the tea-bowls, cups and saucers, and the figures were usually very neat—very unlike New Hall. Early in the nineteenth century the blue crossed 'L's' mark 𝓛 was introduced and used alone or with the pattern number beneath.

The standard shapes of these early services are shown in Plates 202, 203 and 204. The handle on the oval-based straight-sided teapot seems to occur only on Minton wares, although the cream-jug has a Coalport analogue. In the case of the other shape of teapot (Plate 203) the manner in which the handle is attached to the body is also distinctive, but the cream-jug and the covered sugar-pot are less individual: perhaps the bold line of the thumb-rest gives them away. Certainly New Hall rarely used this feature.

Some of the patterns which may be confused are:

Minton pattern 4	New Hall pattern 208
Minton pattern 7	New Hall pattern 195
Minton pattern 18	New Hall pattern 415
Minton pattern 44	New Hall pattern 420
Minton pattern 13	Factory Y pattern 105.

11

THREE UNIDENTIFIED GROUPS
OF PORCELAIN

The commercial manufacture of porcelain was the tantalizing ambition of many Englishmen during the second half of the eighteenth century and the beginning of the nineteenth century. Many of the successful merchants are famous names whose products are recognized and recorded, but many remain anonymous since few marks were used. Either they had little faith in their own success or they feared condemnation for lack of originality.

When the hard-paste patent expired in 1796 numerous Staffordshire potters tried to follow in New Hall's footsteps. The hard-paste body was used or modified and this was potted in similar shapes, decorated with imitative patterns.

It has been possible to record sufficient porcelain to show that three different factories successfully made a New Hall type of tea-service. The most important of them made a wide selection of shapes and applied a full range of decoration: on-glaze enamel, underglaze-blue decoration and fine gilding. Although these pieces can be classified none of them bears a maker's name or mark. It is not known who made them. However, since they are frequently erroneously attributed to New Hall in salerooms, shops and private collections it seems worth publishing my information in its present state. It can serve as a foundation for further research.

In this book they have been given the titles: Factory X, Factory Y and Factory Z.

Of course there are many pieces which remain unclassified. Some of them fall into small groups, but at the present time not enough examples have been found to justify classification in this book.

FACTORY X

Reconstruction of this outline of the output of Factory X, the most prolific of the three unknown factories, has been fascinating detective work. Besides the paste and the glaze, careful attention has been paid to the shapes of the cream-jugs and the teapots as well as to the decoration, that is the pattern and its number; four of the different pedestal jug shapes have been seen in the pink ribbon pattern and marked with the number 126 (The New Hall pattern number is 186, and that found on the wares of Factory Z is 116). A pedestal jug, 'silver-shape' teapot (Plate 227) and a coffee-pot have been seen decorated with the same pattern and all numbered 214. A pedestal jug and a 'silver-shape' jug are recorded (Plate 231) decorated with pattern 235. An oval-based, ogee-waisted teapot in a part tea-service with a 'silver-shape' cream-jug is in the Museum at Cardiff decorated with the same pattern (number 215), and a 'silver-shape' teapot is in the Stoke-on-Trent Museum at Hanley decorated with the same pattern and bearing the same number and even the same workman's mark. The paste of this last group of pieces is different from that used at the beginning of the factory's life.

The first teapot had a simple globular shape and stood on a deep footrim (Plate 215). The handle had a ridge across the top which sometimes curled forward, and the lower terminal of the handle kicked away from the body of the pot, a feature seldom found on New Hall teapots. The lid, which overlapped the collar, was topped with a flask-shaped knob. A very distinctive curved ridge occurs on the end of the spout and this was often picked out by decoration in gold or enamel. Faceted and spiral fluted modifications occur (Plates 214 and 213). On these the lid fits within the collar and the knob may be faceted and grooved.

The globe was followed by the 'silver-shape'; just as was seen with New Hall. The spout retained the curved ridge near the end and its sinuous swan neck shape was heightened by the upper edge following the double curve of the lower edge (the upper edge of the New Hall original was almost a straight line with little inflection). Reeded and spiral fluted variants were made (Plates 223 and 222). In the latter case, unlike the New Hall original, the straight vertical ridges found on the plain teapot were not retained as upright pillars between the sections of curved flutes.

Eventually, as at many contemporary factories, an oval-based ogee-waisted teapot was introduced (Plate 233). This started with a plain loop handle but when this was changed to a heavy scroll the lack of rhythm in the overall shape was emphasized (Plate 235). The impression given by these teapots is that the factory was on the decline.

The two illustrated coffee-pots (Plates 219 and 230) belong to different periods of the factory's life. The reeded pot is an early specimen with a hard grey paste and very shiny glaze, the knob and the mark on the end of the spout being typical. The body shape of the other pot is less elegant, the paste and glaze are duller and the decoration has less character.

Pedestal cream-jugs were made in a variety of shapes (Plates 221, 227 and 228), most of which were quite different from those made by New Hall. Their principal feature was the ridge across the top of the handle. So far as my knowledge of this factory goes, they did not make jugs without this ridge. On the other hand, New Hall made none with it. The New Hall overlapping thumb-rest bears no resemblance to it.

Although the 'silver-shape' cream-jugs can also be identified by their handles their general proportions are different from those of the New Hall original and also from those of Factory Y. These are illustrated in Plate 237, where the fullness of the spout, the curve of the shoulder and the shape of the body appear to be distinctive. Like New Hall, this factory made two sizes of jug.

Tea-bowls and saucers, which in the early years were neatly potted, are hard to identify with certainty although they are readily distinguished from New Hall wares. The glaze in particular is softer and much more shiny, often showing a rippled orange-peel-like surface. This is particularly noticeable on the saucers and plates. There is often glaze on the bottom of the footrim, and within the footrim there are few gas bubbles.

Coffee-cups during the early years had a very characteristic handle which is pointed at the top rather like an imp's ear (Plate 218). Plain, reeded, faceted and spiral fluted variants were made and it is these latter which seem to have the most distinctive shape. New Hall's spiral fluting always seems to be even and leisurely, an effect produced by the two curves having the same radius so that the top end of any one ridge was almost above the bottom end, and the cup was slightly waisted. The curves used by other factories always have a smaller radius and the ridges are sharper. The final product thus has a much crisper appearance. The forward and backward curves of these non-New Hall pieces do not have the same radius, with the result that the top end of a given ridge is not directly above the bottom end. In the products of both Factory X and Factory Y the top end of a ridge is noticeably to the right of the bottom end. This is caused, in the former case, by having a tighter curve of smaller radius at the bottom than at the top and the cup being waisted (Plate 246).

The wares already described have formed the basic essentials for a tea- or coffee-set, and in general these are all that appear to have been made. Except for teapot-stands which matched the teapot shape and size (usually being slightly broader than the New Hall counterpart) the only other pieces which I have seen have been covered sugar-pots and spoon-trays. The round sucrier (Plate 224) was in a service the teapot of which was of 'silver-shape', and the spiral fluted sucrier (which had no ring handles) also accompanied a 'silver-shape' teapot. The spoon-trays so far seen have been either like a small 'silver-shape' teapot stand or of oval shape. In both cases, unlike New Hall specimens, they were glazed underneath.

This, then, is a description of the potting shapes given to tea-services made by this unknown factory. It shows an ambitious start with a later decline. Probably more specimens will be identified and it would not be surprising to find a new range of products made in bone-china.

The style of decoration shows a similar development. Restrained gilding of a good quality is seen on the first products as well as enamels. The latter lacked the brightness of the first New Hall palette but were similar to that in use after about 1790. Later (for example, on patterns 323 and 325) a dull yellow and orange-red were introduced to the palette, and black was used in many patterns. In fact, the whole effect was rather dingy. To complete the range of decoration an underglaze cobalt blue was used (Plate 229). This occurs in hand-painted patterns but not, to my knowledge yet, in transfer-prints. Possibly the blue colour was unsatisfactory or else by this date there was little demand for blue-and-white porcelain tea-wares.

The paste and glaze used for the globular teapots and the first 'silver-shape' teapots were very similar to the New Hall hard-paste. In the two samples tested, the paste gave exactly the same electron diffraction patterns as New Hall and the hard-paste Coalport bodies. In all of them crystals of the mineral mullite were present. The bodies are indistinguishable by transmitted light, but the glazes are different. The glaze for this unknown factory is softer than New Hall's and possibly contains more lead, added as a flux. This also could account for its being more shiny. The glaze obviously flowed over the biscuit body better than the New Hall glaze, giving a thin close-fitting cover. Rarely were there pools of surplus glaze and there were few visible bubbles. However, in the middle of the factory's life the paste changed to a whiter and more translucent appearance which was due to the addition of bone ash (chemical tests for the presence of phosphates have been positive). When looked at against a strong light the paste exhibits a most characteristic blue-green colour, a strong duck-egg colour, nothing like the Worcester green.

It is difficult to suggest a definite date for the porcelain of this factory. If the New Hall patent was enforced then production must have begun in 1796 or soon afterwards. If the average output of different patterns was similar to that of New Hall—that is, 30 to 35 per annum—then the change of paste occurred after about eight years' production, which would be the time when bone ash was being introduced by other Staffordshire potters following in Spode's footsteps. The deterioration in shape and decoration would also be consistent with this period of production although it seems more likely to be due to a lack of inspiration and leadership.

Unfortunately the potting shapes do not support this picture. Globular teapots belong more to the 1780's than the 1790's and the oval ogee-waisted teapot was made by most other factories in 1795 rather than in 1805. The only hypothesis on which these earlier dates would be possible would be that New Hall allowed this factory to use the raw materials under licence. It is said that 'the most extensive and profitable branch of the New Hall business was the making and vending of the glaze called "composition", made according to Champion's specification . . .'.[1] If this is true, then they could also have sold the raw materials for the body. It is a logical step, since the composition of the body and glaze must be carefully matched for successful porcelain manufacture.

Unfortunately, again, there is no evidence to show that New Hall allowed anyone to make porcelain from their growan-stone and china-clay, and why should they? It is against human nature to allow a monopoly to be shared.

Another possibility is that hard-paste porcelain was made by Anthony Keeling and John Turner after their withdrawal from the partnership. It could be that when they left they retained the right to use the raw materials to make porcelain. However, I have seen only one piece of porcelain which was probably made by Keeling and this was certainly not hard-paste.

The case for John Turner is stronger. He was a very skilful potter and he made porcelain. The early products of this unknown factory are certainly worthy of his name. Their potting shapes would also agree with a date of production soon after his withdrawal from the New Hall Company. Turner died in 1787 and although his sons successfully carried on the business the quality of the products gradually deteriorated. Again this fits in with the outline history of Factory X. A few pieces of porcelain with the impressed mark 'TURNER' are known, but their body and glaze are not really like those of the present wares. Not a single marked piece has turned up amongst the products of Factory X and it is difficult to believe that John Turner would have made so many pieces without adding his mark to one of them.

[1] Llewellyn Jewitt, op. cit., vol. 2, p. 306.

THREE UNIDENTIFIED GROUPS OF PORCELAIN

The problem of identity remains. Here is a factory which made porcelain for at least fifteen years (probably between 1796 and 1810), and left no recognisable marks upon its wares. It is possible that it worked in Liverpool but it seems more likely to have Staffordshire origins. Like New Hall, it made an ambitious start producing porcelain of very good quality and decoration. As with many other factories which started about this time, the initial impetus was not maintained and the quality of production degenerated.

SOME PATTERNS AND THEIR NUMBERS USED BY FACTORY X

Pattern 112 (Plate 216)
Similar colouring and style to New Hall pattern 171.

Pattern 114 (Plate 217)
Borders: Mauve line inside the jug and pink line outside. Main spray: Pink rose within a mauve feathery frame. Green leaves.

Pattern 125 (Plate 218)
Borders: Pink scale from an iron-red line. Three blue leaves hang from each patch of scale. Florets separate the pink scale patches. Undulating iron-red line crossing a straight iron-red line with blue and green leaves and coloured florets attached to them. Main spray: Single pink rose.

Pattern 126 (Plates 219 and 220)
Similar colouring and style to New Hall pattern 186. Pattern 116 of Factory Z is also similar.

Pattern 135 (Plate 221)
Border: Magenta line with pink scale patches attached. Three blue leaves hang from the patches of scale. Linking chains are of green and brown leaves and pink roses. Main spray: Single pink rose.

Pattern 145
Similar colouring and style to New Hall pattern 195. Factory Z used this pattern and so did Herculaneum. This latter factory gave it the number 189.

Pattern 152 (Plates 222, 223 and 224)
Decoration all gold.

Pattern 212 (Plate 225)
Border: Mauve scrolls join pink roses with red-brown stamens. Main spray: Pink rose. The other bud is pale green with pink streaks.

Pattern 213 (Plate 226)

Border: Magenta loops are alternately interrupted by a blob and two dots in blue and a semi-circular floret within an angular iron-red frame. Main spray: Single pink rose.

Pattern 214 (Plate 227)

A two-colour pattern in pink and mauve.

Pattern 221 (Plate 228)

Border: Two thin iron-red lines with blue dots in between. Magenta swags with alternate pink roses and carmine florets between. Main spray: Single pink rose.

Pattern 235 (Plate 231)

Borders: Magenta zigzag line between two thin black lines. Narrow chain line coloured green between black lines. Main spray: Pink rose and pale green leaves tied with a blue ribbon line.

Pattern 312 (Plate 232)

Border: The sequence of flowers is a pink rose, pink and blue bud and a pink and yellow floret. When this pattern is applied to a teapot it is placed around the lid and on the top horizontal shoulder of the pot. There is no spray used in this pattern, only scattered sprigs.

Pattern 315 (Plate 233)

Border: Pink swags link the green outlines of the medallions. The florets in the border are mostly iron-red and magenta and give an overall messy appearance.

Pattern 323 (Plate 234)

Border: Thin black line from which hang triangles painted alternately with yellow centres inside an orange-red band and orange-red within an outer yellow band. Beneath is a leafy line bearing alternately a pink rose and a blue flower. There is no main spray.

Pattern 325 (Plate 235)

Border: Between two black lines each strip of the zigzag consists of two orange-red and one yellow section. The florets in the border have five pink petals around a yellow centre. There is no main spray, only enamel coloured sprigs.

Pattern 347 (Plate 236)

The decoration is in iron-red and puce.

Pattern 357 (Plate 237)

Orange-coloured enamel decoration. This is similar in colour and style to New Hall pattern 295. Other factories used this pattern and colour under the numbers 22 and 164.

FACTORY Y

Factory Y appears to have made only tea- and coffee-services based on the 'silver-shape' teapot, plain and with spiral fluting. Probably it made reeded variants as well, but they have not yet been identified. When compared with New Hall wares there are some similar patterns which have different numbers, as well as cases where a given pattern number is found associated with different patterns for the two factories. Although in some cases the paste and glaze used are very similar to those used by New Hall, there are numerous differences in the shapes of the wares. That provides sufficient evidence for the exclusion of this group of porcelain from the production of New Hall.

On the other hand, it is possible that these pieces were made by Factory X, for none of the pattern numbers or patterns so far found are discrepant. But the spiral-fluted 'silver-shape' teapots of these two factories are so different, as also are the appearance of the paste and glaze, that it seems there must have been two different manufacturers.

Analysis using X-ray diffraction patterns suggests that a hard-paste body was made, and this indicates that Factory Y began after 1796. The highest pattern number recorded is 163, which suggests a working life of less than ten years. There are two possibilities here: either the firm closed down after this short life or else it changed over to making bone-china using an entirely new range of shapes. This change could have been made at any time during the first decade of the nineteenth century and would fit into the present outline development. However, if the firm did change to the manufacture of bone-china then it did so abruptly and with little overlap of potting style.

It is difficult to identify the products of this factory by studying the appearance of the paste and glaze alone, since their composition was very similar to that pioneered by New Hall. I think the glaze was softer than the New Hall glaze so that there are more signs of rubbing and wear on pieces, especially on the fluted saucers. The glaze tends to be more glossy and there are few gas bubbles in it.

The only true guide is the shape of the larger pieces of a service. Tea-bowls and saucers can offer no special feature and although many of the coffee-cups have a small curled piece on the top of the handle this feature occurs also on Miles Mason's cups. The sharpness and shape of spiral fluting is markedly different from that of New Hall (Plate 246).

The teapot is the key piece. The spout is very much like a swan's neck. Its upper line is 's'-shaped following the lower line, a feature which distinguishes it from the New Hall counterpart. Although it is octagonal in cross-section the faces do not meet at sharp angles and at the top and the bottom adjacent faces almost merge. The full looped handle is different from the standard New Hall flattened or pushed-in loop. The lid usually has a deep ring to hold it in the opening of the pot and the knob has its own characteristic shape. It is a strawberry on the fluted teapot lid (New Hall's is a pine-cone) and shows a rather inelegant lumpiness on the plain lid.

Factory Y featured the 'silver-shape' teapot (Plate 239), and frequently imposed spiral curved fluting upon the original shape (Plate 240). The manner in which this was done was distinctive. Whereas New Hall retained the four straight vertical ridges which are the characteristic feature of the 'silver-shape' teapot, Factory Y like Factory X allows these ridges to follow the line of the spiral fluting. It is hard to decide which is the better style. When the ridges are straight the teapot retains a firm upright shape; when they are curved the teapot appears to be leaning backwards, almost as though a good push would make it fall over. The quality of some of these pots compares very favourably with the best of New Hall.

A small 'silver-shape' cream-jug accompanied the teapot (Plate 245). Its shape was more upright and the ridges were more sharply defined than on the similar jug made by New Hall. The loop of the handle is small and the bottom of the handle joins the body at the shoulder much higher up than on the New Hall original. The spiral fluted version has a completely different rhythm and like the coffee-cup has a slightly curled ridge across the top of the handle (Plate 241).

Although some of the patterns were copied from New Hall they are usually (except for pattern number 104) neatly painted and some are quite delightful (pattern numbers 121 and 129). The principal decoration was usually either a pair or a group of flowers, like New Hall but unlike Factory X. Most teapots had some decoration on the spout and the handle, but too much importance must not be given to these. It is very easy to be misled or to jump to wrong conclusions. However, some features occur often enough to be worth mentioning and considering as supplementary evidence for attribution. Frequently but not always there was a line around the base of the spout where it joined the pot (New Hall only did this with gilt decoration), and a line half way up the collar around the lid opening and even half way up the knob on a plain teapot lid. None of the pieces seen bears a factory mark but there seems to be one painter's mark which occurs frequently. It looks like a letter 'S' or a number '5' written backwards. These decorative points must be used with caution and discretion.

SOME PATTERNS AND THEIR NUMBERS USED BY FACTORY Y

Pattern 101 (Plate 238)

Border: Iron-red zigzag lines between two blue lines interrupted by a blue motif within a magenta frame. Main spray: A broad green leaf between a pink and a mauve rose.

The main spray is similar to that used by New Hall in pattern 208.

Pattern 104 (Plate 239)

This is a poor copy of New Hall's pattern 20 with a different border. Two connected rectangles, sometimes in black and sometimes in iron-red, interrupt a dotted line between two thin black lines.

Pattern 105 (Plate 240)

Border: Blue rim line with an iron-red line below. From this latter hangs a series of pink scale blobs edged with yellow and connected by blue dotted loops and pink roses. Main spray: Back-to-back pink and mauve roses.

This pattern is the same as Minton pattern 13.

Pattern 111 (Plate 241)

Border: A line of blue arrow-heads crossed by an undulating line of orange dots. Main spray: A broad green leaf between a pink and a mauve rose.

This pattern is similar to pattern 101 of this factory and pattern 208 of New Hall.

Pattern 121 (Plate 242)

Border: The undulating line is magenta with magenta leaves alternating with iron-red dotted florets with four green leaves. The line above is black. Main spray: A pink rose back-to-back with a mauve petalled auricula (yellow centre) with a small pink rose rising out of the spray.

Pattern 127 (Plate 243)

Border: Pink scale band interrupted by small coloured sprigs beneath a line of magenta arrow-heads between two black lines. Main spray: The spray of flowers spreads around a central magenta flower and is set in a brown bowl with a blue ribbon beneath.

Pattern 129 (Plate 244)

Yellow enamel rim lines. Main spray: A well painted flower spray featuring a pink rose, mauve freesia and small iron-red and yellow flowers.

FACTORY Z

Factory Z made its own distinctive shape of teapot which I have called 'bucket-shape' (Plate 248). Since it bears no resemblance to any known New Hall teapot it is surprising to find it attributed so frequently to that factory. The reason is, I suppose, that most patterns seen on them are of the New Hall style. In particular, one of the most commonly found patterns (numbered 116) is similar to the New Hall pink ribbon pattern (number 186).

Some of the early patterns incorporate gilding (pattern number 52 being similar to New Hall's number 89) and a number are in black monochrome. One very attractive pattern (number 90) is a black stipple print of a three-masted sailing ship and two men upon a foreground cliff. The picture is within a gilt circle. Nevertheless, most patterns use coloured enamels in a New Hall style. Some show a distinctive painter's hand, neat outline brushwork for the sprays, and the borders painted with fine, almost pen-like strokes. Pattern number 130 is a good example (Plate 252).

The largest part of the output of Factory Z is the tea-service featuring the bucket-shape teapot. The covered sucrier (Plate 247) has an obvious family resemblance and the cream-jug (Plate 251) a similar rhythm. The handles on both the teapot and the cream-jug were attached to the body in a characteristic way. The upper, rather pointed, terminal was stuck on to the teapot without much attempt to round the edges or smooth it into the body. This feature became more pronounced on later cream-jugs (Plates 256 and 257).

The oval-based teapot with vertical sides was very similar to the product of many other factories (Plate 252). The features which seem to distinguish it are the slight inward curve of the sides towards the top and the way in which the lid fits deeply into the opening. The spout was attached very low down on the body and the base was quite flat and unglazed.

Since the teapot handle had an outward kink near the bottom, it is rather surprising to find the matching cream-jug with a plain loop handle (Plates 256 and 257). The upper handle-body joint always showed the thick overlap, and the base, like that of the teapot, was usually flat and unglazed.

This manufacturer seems to have experimented with the body composition, since its appearance varies. There are times when it seems very white and covered with a soft, bright glittering glaze;

at other times it is more cream-coloured beneath a bright soft, rippled glaze. Usually the translucency to bright light is brown and frequently poor owing to the density of the paste, which has a very soft appearance.

It is often claimed that New Hall made earthenware but I have yet to be convinced of this. However, Factory Z did. Some of the bucket-shaped teapots are earthenware, and some of these bear the same pattern (and appropriate pattern number) as the similar porcelain specimen. Such a chain of evidence has not been produced for New Hall yet.

Porcelain made by this factory was usually marked only with a pattern number and, like New Hall, these numbers are found on the larger pieces of a service. When the marked piece was an open sugar-basin or a slop-bowl, the pattern number was often on the inside of the footrim. Whereas a pattern number is normally read by looking at it from the centre of a piece, with this factory the numbers are frequently the other way round and must be read from the outside.

No piece marked with a maker's name has yet turned up but a number of teapots bear an impressed circle. Usually this is found beneath the outer edge of the lid and sometimes also on the shallow footrim of the base. It is possible that this is a mark for matching the teapot and its lid: on the other hand, this mark is found alone and together with 'MASON' impressed in the shallow footrim of some of Miles Mason's teapots and cream-jugs. Could this Factory Z then really be the early products of Miles Mason in Staffordshire or in Liverpool? It is a possibility, but there is no proof. The oval-based, straight-sided teapot could be the link but it was a common contemporary shape as has already been shown. The porcelain body of this factory is light-weight, and both warm and soft to the touch, quite unlike the usual Mason body, which was cold, compact and heavy.

SOME PATTERNS AND THEIR NUMBERS USED BY FACTORY Z

Pattern 4 (Plate 247)
   A copy of New Hall pattern number 173.

Pattern 52 (Plate 248)
   The decoration is all gold except for magenta triple lines which divide the star-filled ovals.
   This pattern is similar to New Hall pattern 89.

Pattern 90 (Plate 249)
   The decoration and border are all black.

Pattern 116 (Plates 247 and 250)

Both the border designs are very similar to New Hall pattern 186, the pink ribbon pattern, but the spray in this case is a pink and mauve back-to-back rose.

Pattern 126 of Factory X is also similar.

Pattern 130 (Plates 251 and 252)

Borders: The narrow chain one is an outline in black washed over with a light green. The wide one is an iron-red undulating line between two black lines and interrupted by iron-red and black octagons. An undulating mauve dotted line is beneath. Main spray: An open mauve flower with two iron-red flowers, interspersed with light green leaves, growing beyond it. On either side are a pink and a mauve rose.

Pattern 132 (Plate 253)

Borders: Narrow one is a sequence of purple arrow-heads. The wide one is a series of pairs of iron-red rectangles between two black lines with an undulating black dotted line beneath. Main spray: Magenta daisy with a yellow centre and a yellow flower bud growing to the right of it.

Pattern 138 (Plate 254)

Borders: Pink dotted circles on a pink wash band with an undulating black dotted line beneath. The other border device is in magenta. Main spray: A pink-red flower from which grows a pair of blue spikes of buds with a green leaf between.

Pattern 140 (Plate 255)

Borders: Undulating dotted black line beneath a brown line. A sequence of ovals and pairs of dots in blue. Main spray: An orange-brown vase outlined with black containing two pink roses and with a blue ribbon on the left of it.

Pattern 152 (Plate 256)

Decoration all in black.

Pattern 179 (Plate 257)

Brown rim lines. The flowers have petals in two shades of brown and yellow centres.

BIBLIOGRAPHY

BOOKS

W. A. Pitt, *Topographical History of Staffordshire*, 1817

Simeon Shaw, *History of the Staffordshire Potteries*, 1829

J. Ward, *The Borough of Stoke-on-Trent*, 1843

H. Owen, *Two Centuries of Ceramic Art in Bristol*, 1873

Llewellyn Jewitt, *The Ceramic Art of Great Britain*, 2 vols., 1878

J. C. Wedgwood, *Staffordshire Pottery and its History*, 1913

H. Eccles and B. Rackham, *Analysed Specimens of English Porcelain*, 1922

F. Severne MacKenna, *Cookworthy's Plymouth and Bristol Porcelain*, 1946

F. Severne MacKenna, *Champion's Bristol Porcelain*, 1947

G. E. Stringer, *New Hall Porcelain*, 1949

R. G. Haggar, *The Masons of Lane Delph*, 1952

R. G. Haggar and W. Mankowitz, *The Concise Encyclopaedia of English Pottery and Porcelain*, 1957

B. M. Watney, *English Blue and White Porcelain of the Eighteenth Century*, 1963

R. J. Charleston (editor), *English Porcelain 1745–1850*, 1965

B. Hillier, *The Turners of Lane End*, 1965

R. M. Barton, *A History of the Cornish China Clay Industry*, 1966

G. A. Godden, *An Illustrated Encyclopaedia of British Pottery and Porcelain*, 1966

G. A. Godden, *Minton Pottery and Porcelain of the First Period 1793–1850*, 1968

ARTICLES

F. H. Rhead, 'New Hall china', *Connoisseur*, vol. XLVI, September–December 1916, pp. 221–4

W. H. Tapp, 'Fidelle Duvivier: ceramic artist', *Apollo*, vol. XXXII, December 1940, pp. 160–3, and ibid., vol. XXXIII, March 1941, pp. 57–9

T. A. Sprague, 'Hard-paste New Hall porcelain', *Apollo*, vol. XLIX, June 1949, pp. 165–7; ibid., July 1949, pp. 16–18; ibid., August 1950, pp. 51–4; ibid., October 1950, pp. 109–12. 'Black transfers on bone-paste porcelain', ibid., vol. LXIII, March 1956, pp. 85–86. 'New light on polychrome Caughley', ibid., vol. LXIX, January 1959, pp. 14–17. 'Hard-paste New Hall porcelain', *English Ceramic Circle Transactions* (*E.C.C. Trans.*), vol. 3, part 3, 1954, pp. 123–8

R. G. Haggar, 'New Hall—the last phase', *Apollo*, vol. LIV, November 1951, pp. 133–7

R. J. Charleston, 'The end of Bristol. The beginning of New Hall: some fresh evidence', *Connoisseur*, April 1956, pp. 185–8

D. F. Holgate, 'Polychrome and hard-paste Caughley porcelain', *English Ceramic Circle Transactions*, vol. 6, part 3, 1967, pp. 268–83

INDEX

PLATES

1. A teapot illustrated by Ll. Jewitt (op. cit., vol. 2, fig. 460) and said to be decorated by Fidelle Duvivier. See pages 35 and 59

2. Early New Hall part tea-service. Note the shape of the handles and the corrugated moulding of the bodies
Decoration sepia and gold; c. 1782; teapot ht. 6 in.
K. L. Prior Esq. See pages 35 and 51

3. Cream-jug decorated in enamels. The moulded leaves are outlined in green with magenta veins. The border has alternate blue and magenta devices. Ht. 3¼ in. See page 50

4. Jug decorated in enamels and inscribed 'Thomas Brundrell 1793'; ht. 6¾ in. City Museum and Art Gallery, Stoke-on-Trent. See page 51

5. Cream-jugs with corrugated moulded bodies and decorated enamels: on the left with pattern 3, ht. 4¼ in.; and on the right with pattern 67; c. 1782–5. See pages 35 and 51

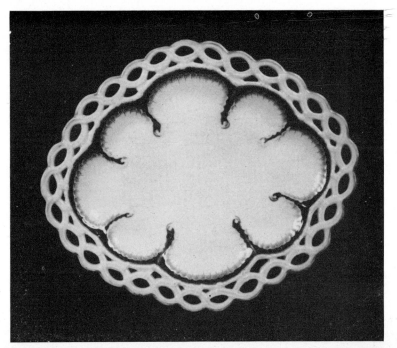

6. Dessert-plate with pierced edge. Dark blue underglaze and gold;
   c. 1782–7; l. 10¼ in. G. E. A. Grey Esq. See page 50
7. Dessert-wares. Bright blue underglaze and gold; c. 1782–7
   Lobed dish: l. 8¾ in. See page 50

8. Teapot decorated with underglaze dark blue band and gold;
c. 1782–7; ht. 6½ in. Mr. and Mrs. A. Thomas. See page 54
9. Jug, cup and tea-bowl decorated with the same underglaze
dark blue band and with different added gold decoration;
c. 1782–7; jug ht. 4¼ in. See page 54

10. Tea-caddy and cover decorated in light blue enamel and gold;
c. 1782–7. G. E. A. Grey Esq. See page 49

11. Tea-caddy and cover decorated in underglaze dark blue and gold;
c. 1782–7; ht. 4¼ in. G. E. A. Grey Esq. See page 49

12. Spoon-trays; c. 1782–7. Left: decorated in underglaze dark blue and gold;
l. 5¾ in. Right: pattern 83. See page 50

13. Jug decorated in enamels by Fidelle Duvivier
Inscribed with the initials 'SD'; c. 1790–1800; ht. 5¾ in.
City Museum and Art Gallery, Stoke-on-Trent. See pages 44 and 59
14. The Fox and Stork fable painted in enamels and gold by Fidelle Duvivier;
c. 1782–7. Borough of Luton Museum and Art Gallery. See page 59
15. Signature of 'F:. Duvivier' on the base of the cup shown in Plate 14
Borough of Luton Museum and Art Gallery

16. Jug decorated in enamels by Fidelle Duvivier; c. 1790–1800;
ht. 9½ in. City Museum and Art Gallery, Stoke-on-Trent
See pages 44 and 59

17. Right to left: pattern 3, pattern 22, pattern 139
Largest jug ht. 4¼ in.; c. 1782–7. See page 42
18. Pattern 20. Teapot (right) ht. 6¾ in.; c. 1782–7. See page 36

19. Pattern 20; c. 1782–7; ht. 4½ in. See page 42
20. Pattern 20. Hot-water-jug; c. 1782–7; ht. 7½ in.
G. E. A. Grey Esq. See page 44
21. Pattern 22; c. 1782–7; ht. 2½ in. See page 42

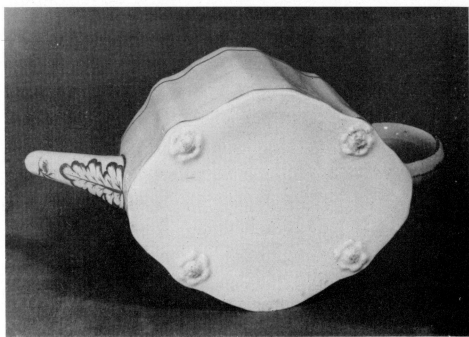

22. Pattern 52. Spoon-tray: c. 1782–7; l. 5¾ in.
23. Base of teapot in Plate 24 showing applied rosette feet and leaf-moulding, outlined with gold, on the underside of the teapot and spout. See page 37

24. Pattern 64. Teapot ht. 5¼ in.; c. 1782–7. See pages 42, 45 and 49

25. Pattern 67; c. 1782–7; ht. 3½ in. See page 42
26. Pattern 78; c. 1782–7; ht. 5¾ in. See page 36
27. Pattern 78. Note the moulding on the handle; c. 1785–9;
ht. 5¾ in. City Museum and Art Gallery, Stoke-on-Trent
See page 37

28. Pattern 83; c. 1782–7; ht. 3¼ in.
G. E. A. Grey Esq. See page 42
29. Pattern 98
30. Pattern 121; c. 1782–7; ht. 7 in. G. E. A. Grey Esq.
31. Pattern 122; c. 1782–7; ht. 3¾ in. See page 42

32. Pattern 133. Teapot-stand; c. 1790–1805; l. 7 in.
33. Pattern 136
34. Pattern 139. Teapot; c. 1786–90; ht. 6 in.
City Museum and Art Gallery, Stoke-on-Trent

35. Pattern 140. Coffee-pot; c. 1782–7; ht. 10 in.
City Museum and Art Gallery, Stoke-on-Trent. See page 41

36. Pattern 141
37. Pattern 142. Covered sucrier: c. 1782–9; ht. 5 in.
City of Liverpool Museum. See page 45

38. Pattern 144. Teapot; c. 1785–90; ht. 5 in. See page 41
39. Pattern 145. Teapot; c. 1787–1800; ht. 7 in.
City Museum and Art Gallery, Stoke-on-Trent. See page 38

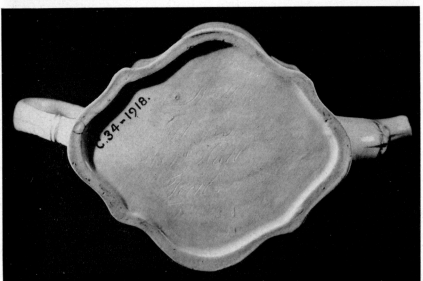

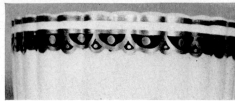

40. Pattern 152. Teapot; c. 1787–90; ht. 6 in.
The unique incised inscription in its base is shown in Plate 41
Victoria and Albert Museum. See page 34
41. Incised inscription in the base of the teapot shown in Plate 40. See page 34
42. Pattern 154   43. Pattern 155

44. Pattern 157   45. Pattern 161   46. Pattern 166
47. Pattern 167. Cream-jug; c. 1782–7; ht. 4 in.
City Museum and Art Gallery, Stoke-on-Trent. See page 42
48. Pattern 168. G. E. A. Grey Esq.
49. Pattern 170. Covered sucrier; c. 1782–9; ht. 5 in.
Mr. and Mrs. A. de Saye Hutton. See page 45

50. Pattern 171. Teapot; c. 1805–14; ht. 4½ in. to the collar
See pages 40 and 56
51. Patterns 171 and 172. Jug (right): c. 1787–95, ht. 4 in.
See page 43

52. Pattern 173. Coffee-pot; c. 1782–7; ht. 9½ in.
Brigadier and Mrs. Victor Hayward. See page 41

53. Pattern 181. Cream-jug; c. 1787–95; ht. 4¾ in.
G. E. A. Grey Esq.
54. Pattern 183. Ht. 2¼ in. This shape of handle was used very
rarely by New Hall; c. 1790. See footnote page 47
55. Pattern 186. Cream-jug; c. 1782–7; ht. 3½ in. See page 42
56. Pattern 191. Teapot; c. 1787–90; ht. 6 in.
City Museum and Art Gallery, Stoke-on-Trent. See page 37

57. Pattern 195. Teapot decorated with a standard pattern
accompanied by a rare dated inscription; ht. 6 in.
A. C. Cater Esq. See page 51
58. Pattern 195. Teapot; c. 1787–90; ht. 6 in.
Dr. Donald Beaton. See page 37

59. Pattern 202. Covered sucrier: c. 1787–90, ht. 5½ in.
See page 45
60. Pattern 202. Covered sucrier: c. 1787–95, ht. 6 in.
See pages 43 and 45

61. Pattern 206. Cream-jug: c. 1787–95, ht. $4\frac{3}{4}$ in.
City Museum and Art Gallery, Stoke-on-Trent
62. Pattern 208. Cream-jug; c. 1790–1805; ht. $4\frac{1}{4}$ in.
63. Pattern 213. Rare covered chocolate-cup; c. 1787–90; ht. $5\frac{1}{4}$ in.
G. E. A. Grey Esq. See page 52

64. Pattern 222. Cream-jug: c. 1790–5, ht. 4¼ in.
Jan Struther, Edinburgh. See page 43
65. Pattern 238. G. E. A. Grey Esq.
66. Pattern 241. Jug; c. 1800; ht. 6¼ in.
City Museum and Art Gallery, Stoke-on-Trent. See page 44

67. Pattern 248   68. Pattern 253   69. Pattern 259   70. Pattern 266

71. Pattern 267
72. Left to right: patterns 272, 490, 274, 856. See page 57
73. Pattern 273. Cream-jug; c. 1790–5; ht. 4¼ in. See page 43
74. Pattern 280

75. Pattern 288   76. Pattern 290   77. Pattern 291
78. Pattern 295. Cream-jug; c. 1790–1805; ht. $4\frac{1}{4}$ in.

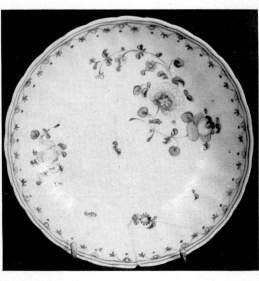

79. Pattern 297. Rare 'silver-shape' tea-caddy; c. 1790–5;
ht. 4¼ in. to the top of the collar
G. E. A. Grey Esq. See page 50
80. Pattern 298
81. Pattern 306. Cream-jug; c. 1795–1810; ht. 3⅞ in.
See page 43
82. Pattern 308

83. Pattern 311. Cream-jug; c. 1787–95; ht. 4½ in. See page 42
84. Pattern 312. Cream-jug; c. 1787–95; ht. 4½ in.
85. Pattern 317
86. Pattern 319. Teapot; c. 1787–1800; ht. 7 in.
City Museum and Art Gallery, Stoke-on-Trent. See page 41

87. Pattern 336. Coffee-pot; c. 1787–1810; ht. 10 in.
See page 41
88. Pattern 338. Cream-jug; c. 1787–95; ht. 4½ in.

89. Pattern 339. Covered sucrier; c. 1787–1800; ht. 6 in.
Mr. and Mrs. P. Wood. See page 45
90. Pattern 343. Covered sucrier; c. 1787–1800; ht. 6 in.

91. Pattern 353. Mug; c. 1787–97; ht. 4½ in.
City Museum and Art Gallery, Stoke-on-Trent. See page 51
92. Pattern 354   93. Pattern 363
94. Pattern 366. Teapot; c. 1790–1805; ht. 6 in.

95. Pattern 367   96. Pattern 373
97. Pattern 376. Cream-jug; c. 1790–1805; ht. $4\frac{1}{4}$ in.
98. Pattern 377. Cream-jug; c. 1790–1805; ht. $4\frac{1}{4}$ in.

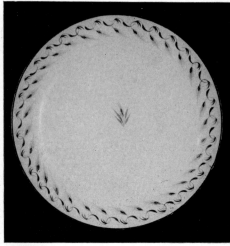

99. Pattern 398   100. Pattern 420. Plate; diam. 8 in.
        101. Pattern 421   102. Pattern 422

103. Pattern 425. Covered sucrier; c. 1795–1805; ht. 5¼ in.
City Museum and Art Gallery, Stoke-on-Trent
See pages 39 and 45
104. Pattern 434. Covered sucrier; c. 1795–1805; ht. 5¼ in.

105. Pattern 437. G. E. A. Grey Esq.   106. Pattern 445
107. Pattern 446. Covered sucrier; c. 1795–1810; ht. 5 in.
108. Pattern 449. Cream-jug; c. 1790–1805; ht. 4¼ in.

109. Pattern 450. Teapot; c. 1790–1805; ht. 6 in.
City Museum and Art Gallery, Stoke-on-Trent
110. Pattern 455
111. Pattern 459. Teapot; c. 1795–1805; ht. 6¼ in.
City Museum and Art Gallery, Stoke-on-Trent. See pages 39 and 41

112. Pattern 461. Teapot with rare fleur-de-lis knob;
c. 1795–1800; ht. 5½ in. See page 39
113. Pattern 462. Teapot; c. 1795–1812; ht. 6 in.
City Museum and Art Gallery, Stoke-on-Trent. See pages 39 and 57

114. Pattern 466. Cream-jug; c. 1795–1805; ht. 4½ in.
G. E. A. Grey Esq. See page 43
115. Pattern 467. Rare two-handled cup; c. 1795–1800; ht. 3½ in.
City Museum and Art Gallery, Stoke-on-Trent. See page 52
116. Pattern 471. G. E. A. Grey Esq.   117. Pattern 472

118. Pattern 480. Cream-jug; c. 1795–1805; ht. 4½ in.
City Museum and Art Gallery, Stoke-on-Trent. See page 43
119. Pattern 499. Cream-jug; c. 1795–1805; ht. 4½ in.
G. E. A. Grey Esq. See page 43
120. Pattern 511
City Museum and Art Gallery, Stoke-on-Trent
121. Pattern 524
122. Pattern 530. Plate; diam. 7¾ in. G. E. A. Grey Esq.

123. Left to right: patterns 533, 631, 737. See page 43
124. Pattern 540. Rare covered chocolate-cup; c. 1795–1800;
ht. 4¼ in. G. E. A. Grey Esq. See page 52
125. Pattern 541. Teapot: c. 1790–1805, ht. 6 in.

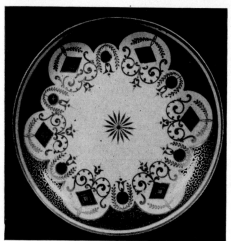

126. Pattern 550. Cream-jug; c. 1795–1805; ht. 4½ in.
G. E. A. Grey Esq.
127. Pattern 562   128. Pattern 575. G. E. A. Grey Esq.
129. Pattern 581. Plate; diam. 7¼ in.

130. Pattern 583. Covered sucrier; c. 1795–1805; ht. 4½ in.
See page 46
131. Pattern 593   132. Pattern 594   133. Pattern 596

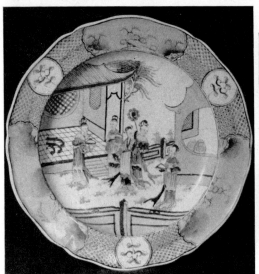

134. Pattern 603. Teapot; c. 1795–1810; ht. 5½ in.
City Museum and Art Gallery, Stoke-on-Trent
135. Pattern 621. Plate; c. 1800; diam. 9 in. See page 50
136. Pattern 662

137. Pattern 686. Cream-jug; c. 1790–1805; ht. 4¼ in.
138. Pattern 692 (left) and pattern 695 (right). See page 46
139. Pattern 746   140. Pattern 748

141. Pattern 779. Teapot; c. 1805–10; ht. 7 in.
Jean Sewell (Antiques) Ltd. See page 39
142. Pattern 827. Covered sucrier; c. 1795–1812; ht. $5\frac{1}{4}$ in.
See page 45

143. Pattern 839. Cream-jug; c. 1790–1805; ht. 4¼ in.
Mr. and Mrs. P. Wood
144. Pattern 901
145. Pattern 914. Teapot; c. 1795–1812; ht. 6 in.
City Museum and Art Gallery, Stoke-on-Trent

146. Pattern 940. Bowl; diam. $6\frac{1}{8}$ in.   147. Pattern 947
148. Pattern 953. Teapot; c. 1795–1810; ht. $5\frac{1}{2}$ in.
Dr. Donald Beaton

149. Coffee-can decorated in gold using Warburton's patented
process; c. 1810–14; ht. $2\frac{1}{2}$ in. Pattern number unknown
See page 58

150. Plate decorated in gold, using Warburton's patented
process, within mazarine blue and gold border;
c. 1810–14; diam. $7\frac{1}{4}$ in.; pattern 846
Victoria and Albert Museum. See page 58

151. Saucer (diam. $5\frac{1}{4}$ in.) and cup whose decoration is mainly
silver lustre. No pattern number appears to have been given
to patterns using this style of decoration; c. 1805–12
See page 55

152. Rare water-jug inscribed: 'John Brown, Yoxall, 1811'
Hard-paste; c. 1811; ht. $5\frac{1}{4}$ in.
G. A. Godden Esq. See pages 32 and 44

153. Pattern 984. Water-jug; bone-china; c. 1815; ht. 5½ in.
City Museum and Art Gallery, Stoke-on-Trent. See page 44
154. Pattern 984. These pieces are bone-china but the pattern is
also found on hard-paste wares; c. 1812–20. Saucer, diam. 5¼ in.
See page 46

155. Pattern 1040. Found on both hard-paste and bone-china wares
156. Pattern 1043. Cream-jug; hard-paste; c. 1795–1815; ht. 3¼ in.
157. Pattern 1045. c. 1805–15; ht. 3¼ in. Although this pattern
is usually found on bone-china, hard-paste pieces are recorded
See page 43
158. Pattern 1046. Plate; hard-paste; c. 1810–14; diam. 7½ in.
159. Pattern 1054. Plate; bone-china; c. 1814–31; diam. 8½ in.

160. Pattern 1058. Bowl; c. 1814–31; diam. 6 in. See page 48
161. Pattern 1064. Milk-jug; c. 1814–31; ht. 3¼ in. See page 44
162. Pattern 1084. Coffee-pot; c. 1814–20; ht. 8¾ in.
Mark: '*New Hall*' within two concentric rings
Victoria and Albert Museum. See page 41

163. Pattern 1084. Rare, two-handled, covered basin;
c. 1814–31; ht. 5 in. See page 53
164. Pattern 1161. Milk-jug; c. 1814–31; ht. $3\frac{1}{4}$ in.
City Museum and Art Gallery, Stoke-on-Trent
165. Pattern 1172. Plate; c. 1814–31; diam. 8 in.
City Museum and Art Gallery, Stoke-on-Trent

166. Pattern 1180. Dr. Donald Beaton
167. Pattern 1373. Teapot-stand; c. 1814–31; l. 7½ in.
City Museum and Art Gallery, Stoke-on-Trent
168. Pattern 1442. Plate; diam. 8½ in.
Mark: '*New Hall*' within two concentric rings
City Museum and Art Gallery, Stoke-on-Trent

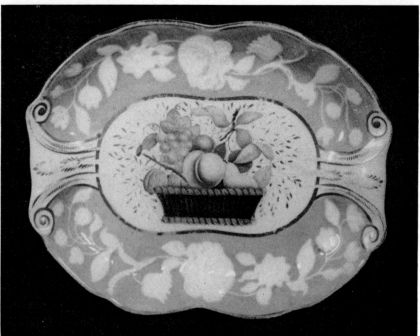

169. Pattern 1478. Rare covered sauce-tureen and fixed stand;
c. 1820–31; ht. 6 in.
National Museum of Wales. See page 53
170. Pattern 1478. Dessert centre dish; c. 1820–31; l. 9¼ in.
Mark: '*New Hall*' within two concentric rings
Rev. and Mrs. Peter Birkett. See page 53

171. Pattern 1480. Dessert-plate with pink ground for the border
and decoration; c. 1820–31; diam. 8 in.
City Museum and Art Gallery, Stoke-on-Trent. See pages 49 and 53
172. Pattern 1485. This shape of cup and handle was used
c. 1820–31; ht. $2\frac{1}{4}$ in. See page 46
173. Pattern 1511. Bowl; c. 1815–31; diam. 6 in.
City Museum and Art Gallery, Stoke-on-Trent. See page 48

174. Pattern 1525. Rare covered chocolate-cup and saucer; c. 1815–31; ht. 6 in.
City Museum and Art Gallery, Stoke-on-Trent. See page 53
175. Pattern 1542. Teapot; c. 1815–31; ht. 6 in.
City Museum and Art Gallery, Stoke-on-Trent

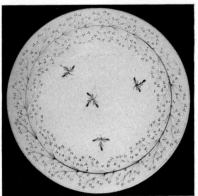

176. Pattern 1547. Milk-jug; c. 1815–31; ht. 3¼ in.
Mark: '*New Hall*' within two concentric rings
City Museum and Art Gallery, Stoke-on-Trent
177. Pattern 1560. Milk-jug; c. 1815–31; ht. 3¼ in.
Mark: '*New Hall*' within two concentric rings
178. Pattern 1623. Saucer; c. 1815–31; diam. 5½ in.
Mark: '*New Hall*' within two concentric rings
179. Pattern 1680. Teapot; c. 1815–31; ht. 6 in.
City Museum and Art Gallery, Stoke-on-Trent. See page 40

180. Pattern 1681. Teapot; c. 1815–31; ht. 6 in.
City Museum and Art Gallery, Stoke-on-Trent
181. Jug decorated in bas-relief with added enamel decoration;
c. 1820–31; ht. 3½ in. Mark: '*New Hall*' within two concentric rings
City Museum and Art Gallery, Stoke-on-Trent. See page 44
182. Jug decorated in white bas-relief on a lavender blue ground;
c. 1820–30; ht. 4¾ in. Mark: '*New Hall*' within two concentric rings
G. E. A. Grey Esq. See page 44

183. Pair of vases decorated mostly with dark blue and gold;
c. 1820–31; ht. 12¼ in. Mark: '*New Hall*' within two concentric rings
City Museum and Art Gallery, Stoke-on-Trent. See pages 53 and 55
184. Smear-glaze teapot; c. 1870–80; ht. 3½ in. Mark: 'NEWHALL',
impressed. This teapot was not made by the New Hall
China Manufactory. It was made by Thomas Booth
when he used the New Hall works
Harris Museum and Art Gallery, Preston. See page 62

185. Part tea-service decorated with underglaze blue transfer-print and gold. The cup has a grooved handle. The teapot (ht. 6¾ in.) and the jug (Mrs. Liane Richards) bear the blue underglaze Frankenthal lion mark; c. 1781–5. See pages 47, 57 and 60

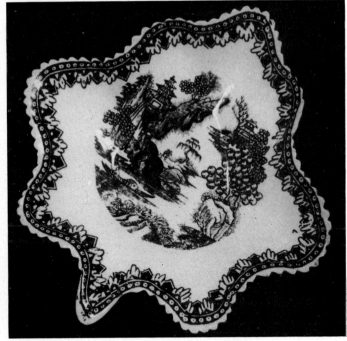

186. Asparagus-server decorated in underglaze blue; c. 1782–7; l. 6¾ in.
G. E. A. Grey Esq. See page 50
187. Knife or fork handle decorated in pale underglaze blue;
c. 1782–7; l. 3⅜ in. See page 50
188. Pickle-dish decorated with underglaze blue transfer-print;
c. 1782–7; l. 6¾ in. G. E. A. Grey Esq. See pages 50 and 57

189. Tea-caddy decorated with underglaze blue transfer-print;
c. 1782–7; ht. 4¼ in. See page 57
190. Cream-jug decorated with underglaze blue transfer-print;
c. 1782–7; ht. 3½ in.
Victoria and Albert Museum. See page 57

191. Covered jug decorated with underglaze blue transfer-print;
c. 1782–7; ht. 5 in. G. E. A. Grey Esq. See pages 42 and 57
192. Covered sucrier decorated with underglaze blue transfer-print;
c. 1785–95; ht. 4¼ in. See page 57

193. Leaf-moulded cream-jugs decorated with underglaze blue
transfer-prints; c. 1782–7; ht. 3¼ in. (left)
G. E. A. Grey Esq. See page 50
194. Coffee-cup and saucer decorated with underglaze blue
transfer-print; c. 1782–7; diam. 5 in. (saucer). See page 57

195. Plate decorated with underglaze blue transfer-print;
c. 1782–95; diam. 8½ in. See page 57
196. Plate decorated with underglaze blue transfer-print;
c. 1790–1810; diam. 8½ in. See page 57

197. Teapot and cream-jug. Pattern 99. Mazarine blue and gold;
Chamberlain's Worcester; c. 1796–1805; ht. 7½ in. (teapot)
See page 89
198. Covered sucrier. Pattern 105. Gold:
Chamberlain's Worcester; c. 1796–1805; ht. 5¼ in.
See page 89

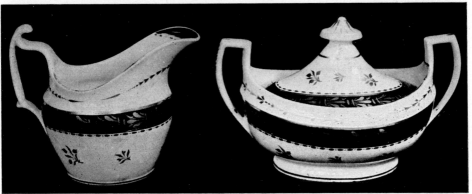

199. Teapot. Pattern 99. Mazarine blue and gold;
Chamberlain's Worcester; c. 1796–1810; ht. 5½ in.
See page 89
200. Covered sucrier and cream-jug. Pattern 99. Mazarine blue and gold;
Chamberlain's Worcester; c. 1796–1810; ht. 5½ in. (sucrier)
See page 90

201. Teapot, jug and plate. The coloured enamels are not so
full in colour as the New Hall pattern 425
Miles Mason; c. 1802–13; ht. 6¼ in. (teapot). See page 94

MINTON

202. Teapot (pattern 105) and milk-jug (pattern 18)
The design and colour of pattern 18 are identical with New Hall's
pattern 415. Minton; c. 1800–10; ht. of jug 3½ in.
G. A. Godden Esq. See page 94

203. Teapot decorated with enamels (pattern 400)
Minton; c. 1810–20; ht. 6¼ in.
Mr. and Mrs. A. de Saye Hutton. See page 94
204. Tea-wares decorated in blue and red enamels and gold (pattern 560)
Minton; c. 1810–20; ht. of covered sucrier 5 in.
G. A. Godden Esq. See page 94

205. Biscuit and glazed wasters excavated at the Caughley
factory site which match the teapot shown in Plate 206;
c. 1796–1805. See page 92
206. Teapot and covered sucrier decorated in enamels
Caughley-Coalport; c. 1796–1805; ht. 6½ in. (teapot)
See page 92

207. Cream-jug decorated in enamels with a copy of New Hall's
pattern 241, with matching sherds found at the Caughley factory site
Caughley-Coalport; c. 1796–1805; ht. 3¾ in.
See page 92
208. Teapot and cream-jug decorated in enamels
Coalport; c. 1800–14; ht. 5¾ in. (teapot). See page 92

209. Teapot decorated in enamels
Coalport; c. 1805–14; ht. 6¾ in.
See page 93
210. Sucrier and cover with matching sherds excavated on
the Caughley factory site
Coalport; c. 1805–14; ht. 5 in.
See page 93

211. Biscuit waster excavated at the Caughley factory site,
between two examples of similar shaped jugs decorated in
enamels (left) and underglaze blue transfer-print (right)
Coalport; c. 1805–14; ht. 4¼ in. See page 93
212. Teacups and coffee-cans with matching sherds
Coalport; c. 1800–14; coffee-cans ht. 2½ in.

213. Teapot decorated in enamels and gold; c. 1796–1805; ht. 6 in.
See page 97
214. Teapot decorated in underglaze dark blue and gold;
c. 1796–1805; ht. 6 in. G. A. Godden Esq. See page 97

215. Teapot decorated in enamels with a pattern resembling
New Hall's pattern 20; c. 1796–1805; ht. 6¾ in.
Harris Museum and Art Gallery, Preston. See page 97
216. Pattern 112. Cream-jug; c. 1796–1805; ht. 3⅛ in.

217. Pattern 114. Jug; c. 1796–1805; ht. 4¼ in.
Mrs. R. L. Ward
218. Pattern 125. c. 1796–1805; teapot ht. 6 in. See page 98

219. Pattern 126. Coffee-pot; c. 1796–1805; ht. 10½ in.
Plymouth City Art Gallery. See page 97
220. Pattern 126. Covered sucrier; c. 1796–1805; ht. 6 in.
221. Pattern 135. Jug; c. 1796–1805; ht. 4¼ in. See page 98

222. Pattern 152. Teapot; c. 1796–1805; ht. 5¾ in.
City Museum and Art Gallery, Stoke-on-Trent. See pages 38 and 97
223. Pattern 152. Teapot; c. 1796–1805, ht. 5¾ in.
G. A. Godden Esq. See page 97

 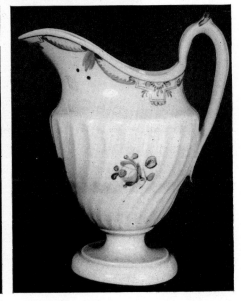

224. Pattern 152. Covered sucrier; c. 1796–1805; ht. 5¼ in.
G. A. Godden Esq. See page 99
225. Pattern 212. Jug; c. 1796–1805; ht. 4½ in.
226. Pattern 213. Jug; c. 1796–1805; ht. 4½ in.

227. Pattern 214. Teapot and cream-jug; c. 1796–1810; ht. 6 in. (teapot)
Mr. and Mrs. T. Edwardson. See pages 97 and 98
228. Pattern 221. Jug; c. 1796–1805; ht. 4½ in. See page 98
229. Teapot decorated in underglaze blue, hand-painted pattern;
c. 1796–1810; ht. 5¾ in. Dr. B. Watney. See page 99

230. Coffee-pot decorated in enamels; pattern number unknown;
c. 1800–10; ht. 9¼ in. See page 97
231. Pattern 235. Jug (right); c. 1800–10; ht. 4½ in. See page 97

232. Pattern 312. Teapot; c. 1800–10; ht. 6 in.
233. Pattern 315. Teapot; c. 1805–10; ht. 7½ in.
National Museum of Wales. See page 97
234. Pattern 323. Jug; c. 1800–10; ht. 3½ in.

235. Pattern 325. Teapot; c. 1805–10; ht. 7 in.
Dr. Donald Beaton. See page 97
236. Pattern 347. Teapot; c. 1805–10; ht. 6 in.
237. Left: New Hall cream-jug; pattern 295; c. 1790–1805; ht. 4¼ in.
Right: Factory X; pattern 357; c. 1800–10; ht. 4 in.
See page 98

238. Pattern 101. Plate; c. 1796–1805; diam. 8 in.
239. Pattern 104. Teapot; c. 1796–1805; ht. 5¾ in.
Mr. and Mrs. A. de Saye Hutton. See page 104
240. Pattern 105. Teapot, c. 1796–1805; ht. 5½ in.
See pages 38 and 104

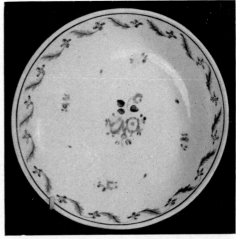

241. Pattern 111. Jug; c. 1796–1810; ht. 3¾ in. See page 104
242. Pattern 121
243. Pattern 127. Teapot; c. 1796–1810; ht. 5½ in.
National Museum of Wales

244. Pattern 129. Teapot; c. 1796–1810; ht. 5¾ in.
245. 'Silver-shape' jugs made by Factory Y (left) and New Hall (right)
Note the different shape of handle and position of rejoining the body
Factory Y jug: c. 1796–1810; ht. 4½ in.
Dr. Donald Beaton. See page 104
246. Three coffee-cups. Factory X (left) decorated in pale blue
enamel and gold, ht. 2½ in.; Factory Y (centre) and New
Hall (right) decorated in enamels. Note the different
curvature of the ridges and the flutes. See pages 98 and 103

247. Covered sucrier (left) decorated in enamels with pattern 4,
and teapot (right) decorated in enamels with pattern 116
Teapot: c. 1800–10; ht. 6 in. See page 106
248. Pattern 52. Teapot; c. 1800–10; ht. 6 in.
City Museum and Art Gallery, Stoke-on-Trent. See page 106

249. Pattern 90. Mr. and Mrs. A. de Saye Hutton   250. Pattern 116
251. Pattern 130. Teapot (porcelain), ht. 6 in.; jug (earthenware);
c. 1800–10. See page 106

252. Pattern 130. Teapot; c. 1800–10; ht. 5¾ in.
Mr. and Mrs. G. Braznell. See page 106
253. Pattern 132. Teapot (earthenware); c. 1800–10; ht. 6 in.

254. Pattern 138   255. Pattern 140
256. Pattern 152. Jug; c. 1800–10; ht. 3¾ in. See page 106
257. Pattern 179. Jug; c. 1800–10; ht. 4 in. See page 106